# What Makes America Tick?

## A Multiskill Approach to English through U.S. Culture and History

Wendy Ashby

Ann Arbor

**The University of Michigan Press**

*This book is dedicated to my family, Dr. Roby Ariew for his mentoring in materials design, and to the memory of my high school history teacher Vicki Greenburg for teaching us to have fun with the past and the present.*

What Makes America Tick?

# Acknowledgments

*Grateful acknowledgments are made to the following authors, collections, publishers, and photographers for permission to use images or to reprint previously published materials.*

DoD Visual Information Record Center for the following photos: the White House (DN-ST-84-08581); the Kremlin (DN-SC-92-04941); the U.S. Army's Berlin Brigade (DF-ST-89-04330); the Vietnam Veterans Memorial (DA-ST-89-01576); the space shuttle (DF-SC-83-09267); the Berlin Wall (DF-ST-91-03564); President Wilson addresses Congress (HD-SN-99-02087); Duke Ellington (HA-SN-99-00410); "We Can Do It!" (HD-SN-99-02457); Marilyn Monroe (HD-SN-99-03125); Confederate lines near Chattanooga Railroad (HD-SN-99-01827); Abraham Lincoln (HD-SN-99-01776); President Johnson greets American troops (HD-SN-99-02054); Tank moves through Saigon (HD-SN-99-02078).

Nancy DeMille of MotoPhoto, Tucson, Arizona, for the photo of the Tucson Human Flag.

Library of Congress, Prints and Photographs Division, for the following photos: Immigrant family looking at Statue of Liberty from Ellis Island (LC-USZ62-50904); Workers in Canton Glass Works, Marion, Indiana (LC-USZ62-105656); A suffragist works to win the vote (LC-USZ62-23622); Representative with flappers doing the Charleston (LC-USZ62-93721); Young man in dustbowl (LC-USF34-009872-E); A migrant mother (USZ62-95653); Woman and two children (LC-USF34-009749-E); Teens learn rock 'n' roll (LC-USZ62-125429); Teenage girls and Elvis movie poster (LC-USZ62-114912); Martin Luther King, Jr. (LC-USZ62-126559); Poster for Woodstock Festival (LC-USZC4-5198).

Ms. Foundation for Women for the artwork "Ms. Foundation for Women: Take Our Daughters to Work®."

National Organization for Women, Inc., for photos from NOW's "1997 Young Feminist Summit." Reprinted by permission of the National Organization for Women, photos by Susan Mackenzie.

# Contents

**To the Instructor**      ix

**To the Student**      xi

**1**    **The U.S. as It Welcomes the 20th Century: The Rise of Large Industry and a Cry for Social Reform**      1

*The Jungle* by Upton Sinclair

Language Focus: Practicing Description

Link to Today: College Drinking—What's So Special about a Fake ID?

**2**    **The U.S. between World Wars: The Roaring Twenties, Black Tuesday, and Beyond**      22

WPA Photography

Language Focus: Using Backchanneling Strategies

Link to Today: The Social Security Debate—Who Will Pay for the Young When They Get Old?

**3**    **The U.S. after World War II: Consumer Culture, Suburbia, and the Baby Boom**      44

Pop Art by Andy Warhol

Language Focus: Using Hedging Techniques

Link to Today: Credit Card Companies on College Campuses—How Much Is Too Much?

**4** **The U.S. at Midcentury: Desegregation and the Demand for Equality and Civil Rights** 61

"I Have a Dream" by Dr. Martin Luther King, Jr.

Language Focus: Using Parallelism

Link to Today: Affirmative Action and College Admissions—Who Should Go to College?

**5** **The U.S. Counterrevolution of the Sixties: Sex, Drugs, and Rock 'n' Roll** 79

*On the Road* by Jack Kerouac

Language Focus: Using Less Direct Speech

Link to Today: Sex Education at School—Contraception or Abstinence?

**6** **The U.S. in the Cold War Era: Defending Democracy from McCarthy to Vietnam** 95

"Like Emily Dickinson," a Poem from the Vietnam War Women's Memorial Project

Language Focus: Understanding Poetry and Figurative Meaning

Link to Today: Campus ROTC—Who Are Those Students in Uniform?

**7** **The U.S. in the Seventies: Women, the Feminist Movement, and the ERA** 119

Billie Jean King's Autobiography

Language Focus: Using Quoted vs. Reported Speech

Link to Today: Take Our Daughters to Work Day—What Is the Future for Girls?

**8** **The U.S. as It Looks toward the 21st Century: Diversity vs. Unity in the New Millennium** 136

The Franklin D. Roosevelt Memorial Wheelchair Statue

Language Focus: Using Compare and Contrast Transition Words

Link to Today: Equal Access on Campus—Can Everybody Have a Share?

**Comments and Suggestions for the Teacher** 157

**Answer Key** 165

# To the Instructor

I designed *What Makes America Tick?* as a comprehensive package of instructional materials for intermediate-level ESL/EFL courses as a bridge into simple advanced skills. I designed it for instructors like you who care about teaching the four skills of reading, writing, speaking, and listening within an authentic context in which culture, vocabulary, and sociolinguistic appropriateness are also stressed and the relationships between all elements of language are explored. My controlling philosophy while producing these study materials was that lower-proficiency language students should be offered the opportunity to study language as it is applied to higher-level thinking activities and that such activities can be based on cultural artifacts such as art, music, literature, and history of the target culture. These higher-level topics have traditionally been reserved for those students who "already" possess advanced-level vocabulary and structures.

The objectives of the study materials are to:

- Advance reading skills by engaging learners in intermediate-level readings pertaining to some important events in modern U.S. history.
- Increase learner proficiency in high-frequency vocabulary words and their derivatives.
- Advance formal and informal writing skills via personal responses to events portrayed in the text and in optional journal keeping.
- Improve formal presentation, informal discussion, and personal speaking skills in class discussions and more structured peer interview situations.
- Enhance listening skills via peer and instructor interaction.

- Expose learners to and provide practice opportunities for sociolinguistically appropriate usages of U.S. American English.
- Provide interaction with authentic cultural artifacts from the 20th century including literature, poetry, artwork, sculpture, photography, speeches, etc., and make explicit their contextual importance.
- Create opportunity for learning and putting into practice a working knowledge of some of the important historical events of the 20th century as well as an understanding of their relationship to current U.S. American institutions, politics, attitudes, and values.

*What Makes America Tick?* consists of eight units, each containing an intermediate-level reading; authentic photos; vocabulary lists and activities; various cloze and open response activities for reading, speaking, listening, and writing; and a "Link to Today" section that examines the current effects of history on younger target language speakers. Additional activities and individual project ideas are available on the book's Web site <www.press.umich.edu/esl>.

I have made it a point to engage students in meaningful, cross-cultural comparisons of politics, attitudes, and values with the aim of eliciting their observations and reactions regarding various policies, movements, and events in U.S. American history, as well as having them engage in meaningful, communicative information-gap activities. It was not possible to include every significant historical event in the 20th century, so the focus is on those events with cultural implications throughout the century and ones with the most far-reaching social implications on ESL students.

Despite my efforts to make this text as culturally rich and authentic as possible, copyright constraints made it difficult to include many things that I think students would enjoy. For this reason, links to sources for materials such as the Andy Warhol artwork (Unit 3) and the Martin Luther King, Jr., speech (Unit 4) as well as other helpful resources are also available on the Web site. In addition, I strongly encourage you to depart from my materials at any time to include other realia that could not be included in the book. My teacher's heart will rest happy knowing that you are out there teaching the materials that I could not include as an author and engaging the students in ways that simply were not feasible via the medium of a textbook. Help them understand what makes America tick!

# To the Student

Hello! I designed *What Makes America Tick?* especially for you intermediate and high-intermediate ESL students. Just like you, I got sick of those boring, sometimes childish English books and so, with the help of the University of Michigan Press, I decided to do something about it. I wanted to give students like you a fun and intellectual way to study English and U.S. American culture and history.

The title of the book is an English idiom. It refers to old-fashioned watches that made a ticking sound. The moving parts inside the watch *made it tick.* When you want to know what makes someone tick, it means that you are puzzled or curious about this person and want to know how this person thinks, feels, and operates. As an ESL student, you are probably curious to find out how the average U.S. American citizen thinks, feels, and operates and why. I hope these materials will help you to better understand why Americans do what they do—what makes them tick.

The objectives of the book are for you to:

- Gain better reading skills through interesting texts.
- Learn new, high-frequency vocabulary words.
- Gain better formal and informal writing skills.
- Gain more advanced speaking and presentation skills.
- Improve your listening skills in peer interviews.
- Learn and practice appropriate uses of U.S. American English.
- Examine authentic cultural artifacts such as: literature, poetry, artwork, sculpture, photography, speeches, etc., and understand why they are important to U.S. Americans.

- Gain a working knowledge of the history of the United States in the 20th century and the important events that shaped current U.S. American politics, institutions, values, and attitudes.

*What Makes America Tick?* has eight units. Each unit contains a reading activity, vocabulary exercises, authentic photos, and activities for reading, speaking, listening, and writing. I will ask you to compare this information with information from your culture and community. Cultural artifacts such as pieces of art, literature, songs, and photos will help you to gain knowledge about past and present life in the United States. I designed this book with the hope that you can enjoy learning about the U.S. and improve your English at the same time. So, work hard and have fun!

## *Net Surfers*

See what information you can find by searching for the following phrase on the World Wide Web: History of the United States since 1865 Syllabus. You will find listings and Web sites for undergraduate college courses and on-line history projects. Many, including those at community colleges, are on-line course notes providing concise summaries and interesting photos and are very accessible to ESL/EFL students. Make sure to look at History 132 at Mesa State University.

## *Presidential Suite*

Try searching for this site on the World Wide Web: IPL POTUS (Presidents of the United States). It contains biographies and home pages for every United States president.

## *Music Box*

### "We Didn't Start the Fire" - Billy Joel

A fast-paced hit from the 1980s, taking the listener chronologically through multiple aspects of post–World War II history

## *At the Movies*

### *Forrest Gump*

A quirky look at United States history through the eyes of a character named Forrest Gump. Experience his boyhood of the 1950s, his coming of age in the 1960s and '70s, and his life as a baby boomer in the 1980s and '90s.

# 1 The U.S. as It Welcomes the 20th Century

## The Rise of Large Industry and a Cry for Social Reform

An immigrant family looks at the Statue of Liberty from Ellis Island. (Courtesy Library of Congress.)

## Net Surfers

See what information you can find by searching for the following names, words, and phrases on the World Wide Web.

Child labor in New York City tenements, 1908

College drinking

Electronic Ellis Island

Food and Drug Administration

*The Jungle*

Muckrakers

1930s prohibition

Progressive era immigration

*Pure Food and Drug Act*

Sinclair, Upton

Temperance

Underage drinking

## *Presidential Suite*

Theodore Roosevelt (R) 1901–9
William Howard Taft (R) 1909–13
Woodrow Wilson (D) 1913–21

## Preparing to Read about the Rise of Large Industry and a Cry for Social Reform

Before we begin to learn about life in the United States at the beginning of the 20th century, let's stop and think about our lives in our own communities today. This will help us compare what we know now with what we will be learning about. Without worrying about grammar or perfect English, take a few minutes to write down some thoughts

about living conditions
the size of your hometown
the largest city you have lived in or visited
the living and working conditions of those who live in large cities

about alcohol
the legal drinking age where you live
the laws about drinking and driving
the public opinion on alcohol and alcoholism

about the status of women
> a woman's place in your society
> the laws on women and voting
> the laws on women and birth control

Share what you wrote with a classmate. You should never feel pressure to share information that is too personal, but an open discussion of ideas is very helpful in using and learning a foreign language.

## Learning New Vocabulary about the U.S. as It Welcomes the 20th Century

**agriculture (n)** farming

**condition (n)** a state of being; surroundings

**constitutional amendment (n)** an addition to the U.S. Constitution; new ones can be added with a 2/3 vote by the Senate and the House of Representatives and approval by 3/4 of state governments. The first 10 constitutional amendments are called The Bill of Rights.

**contraceptive (n)** a birth control device

**industrialization (n)** the shift from a society based on agriculture to one based on factory work

**monopoly (n)** when one business or industry has no competition

**muckrakers (n)** name given to newspaper reporters who exposed bad things; refers to the person who cleans horse stalls

**opposition (n)** the state of being against something; action taken against a person or idea

**suffrage (n)** the right to vote

**urbanization (n)** shift from living on farms to living in cities

**wage (n)** pay; money received based on hourly work

**to bribe (v)** to give someone in an official position money to get what you need or to keep from being arrested for breaking the law

**to encourage (v)** to support or to inspire somebody to do something

**to produce (v)** to make or manufacture

**to repeal (v)** to take away or make powerless (law)

**to replace (v)** to take the place of something; one thing exists instead of another

**to support (v)** to help a person or idea with time, money, or other tools

**crowded (adj)** too much of something in too little space

**moral (adj)** good, right, or correct behavior in a society

**progressive (adj)** forward thinking; looking toward the future

**vocal (adj)** outspoken; making yourself heard

## Talking about New Words and Ideas

Although this is a big list of words to learn, they will be important to understanding the reading, so take some time to think and talk about new ideas associated with the new vocabulary. Use your understanding of the new vocabulary words to discuss the following questions with a partner or in a small group. You can make your own list of words in the margin.

1. In the United States, the Constitution has an "elastic clause." This allows the laws to be stretched to meet the needs of the people. For example, if an old law doesn't help people anymore, a new one can be made. Changes to the Constitution can also be made by additions called *amendments.* A new amendment to the Constitution is suggested and voted on by members of Congress in the Senate and the House of Representatives. If 2/3 of the members vote for it, it can become a **constitutional amendment.** The amendment must also be passed by 3/4 of the state governments. There is no limit on how many amendments the Constitution can have. The first ten amendments to the Constitution are called the *Bill of Rights.*

   A. What are the benefits of such a system?
   B. Are there any problems it could cause?
   C. What happens in your community if a law doesn't help people anymore?
   D. Is there a law that you think needs to be changed? What is it? How can the law be made better?
   E. List some words that are related to **constitutional amendment** in your mind.

2. When a person is very outspoken about a problem, he or she is said to be **vocal.** Being vocal is generally thought of positively in U.S. society. People often ask others' opinions and encourage them to speak up for themselves and their concerns.

   A. Since you started studying English, have you noticed U.S. citizens being vocal?
   B. What kinds of issues were they addressing?
   C. Is it always acceptable to be vocal?
   D. Have you ever been vocal about an issue? What was it? What did you say about it and to whom?
   E. List some words that are related to **vocal** in your mind.

3. When a country has increasing numbers of people living in large cities, the country is becoming **urbanized.** The United States experienced urbanization at the turn of the 20th century. Today, the trend is to move housing and businesses into suburbs, often leaving the cities to decay.

   A. What effects of urbanization/suburbanization have you seen or heard about in the U.S. today?
   B. Do you prefer to live in a large city or a smaller town? Why?
   C. What are some advantages of living in a large city? What are some problems?
   D. List some words that are related to **urbanization** in your mind.

4. Newspaper journalists who exposed crime and other problems at the turn of the century were called **muckrakers.** *Muck* is the dirt and waste found in animal stalls. The stories created by the journalists stopped many unethical practices in U.S. American businesses. However, the business owners often felt that the press took away their right to run their businesses without interference. The U.S. Constitution guarantees freedom of the press, so newspapers can publish stories without the government's approval. These opposing views are a large debate in the U.S. today.

   A. Do you think that the U.S. press should have the right to print anything it chooses?
   B. What are the benefits and problems of such a system?
   C. Do you know of places where the press isn't free to publish what it chooses?

D. What do you think about the idea of media freedom?

E. List some words that are related to **muckrakers** in your mind.

## Making Predictions about the Reading

You probably have a very good idea now from your class discussions and the new words you are learning what kinds of information might be coming up in the reading text. Congratulations! Making predictions (right or wrong) is a good step toward better reading in another language and in your own. Without looking ahead at the reading, jot down the ideas you think will be included in the reading text. It doesn't matter right now if your ideas are correct—the comprehension check comes later in the unit.

Now that you have written down your predictions, share your list with another student in the class. Which items on your list are similar to his or hers? Which are different? Which of your classmates' predictions do you think will be correct?

## Reading about the U.S. as It Welcomes the 20th Century

At the dawn of the 20th century, the United States was still a growing country of 46 states. One hundred immigrants per hour were arriving through Ellis Island, (near New York City). Cities grew rapidly. New York was the largest with 3.4 million, and Chicago followed with 1.6 million. U.S. Americans were feeling the effects of **industrialization** and **urbanization.** Although Americans in the 19th century had worked mostly in **agriculture,** they began to live in the cities, work in large factories, and use the new products made there. Automobiles began to **replace** horses on American streets and over a million people had telephones.

However, quick growth and uncontrolled capitalism caused many problems for the United States. Cities were **crowded,** housing **conditions** poor, **wages** low, and working days long. There were no laws against children working, and although leaders such as Mother Jones were working for this goal, many young children spent 12-hour days doing dangerous jobs in

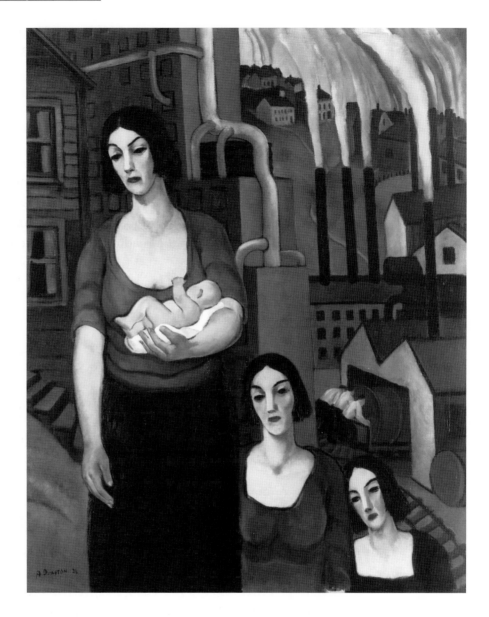

*Industry* (oil on canvas) by Arthur Durston. (Courtesy Smithsonian American Art Museum.)

dirty factories. Profit became more important than the safety of the workers and **monopolies** grew large and powerful. When laws to protect workers were passed, rich factory owners **bribed** officials to look the other way.

In **opposition** to these problems, **progressive** ideas about change began to grow in the middle class. Many newspaper reporters, authors, and social workers focused on the problems of industrialization. Reporters, often called **"muckrakers,"** wrote newspaper stories about children working in the factories. A famous author, Upton Sinclair, wrote *The Jungle* in 1906. The novel exposed the dirty conditions of a Chicago meat-packing

Workers in the Canton Glass Works, Marion, Indiana. (Courtesy Library of Congress.)

factory, **encouraging** the government to pass the *Pure Food and Drug Act* to protect U.S. citizens from unsafe food.

Social workers tried to improve the living conditions in the cities. Seeing many problems caused by alcohol, they began to focus their efforts on making it illegal. Women were especially **vocal** on this front, and their efforts led to the *Prohibition Act* of 1919, a **constitutional amendment** that made **producing,** selling, or drinking alcohol illegal in every state. The Eighteenth Amendment was **supported** by many industrial and religious leaders, who felt that it would help U.S. Americans to be more productive, family-oriented, and **moral.** However, it was expensive to enforce the law, and many people began to make alcoholic drinks in their own homes, creating unsafe alcohol that sometimes caused illness and even death. Illegal alcohol production and sales became big business for gangsters such as Al Capone. Because of the cost and the dangers of private alcohol manufacturing, the law was **repealed** fourteen years later.

The issue of votes for women is known as **suffrage.** Although women were legally able to vote in a few western states, the Nineteenth Amendment, the *Suffrage Act* of 1919, gave women the right to vote nationwide. An 1848 women's conference at Seneca Falls, New York, was the symbolic birthplace of the women's suffrage movement. Elizabeth Cady Stanton and Susan B. Anthony led the movement during the early 1900s. They supported women like Margaret Sanger, who founded the American Birth Control League in 1917. She was arrested and put in jail for giving women information about **contraceptives,** which was illegal.

Efforts of U.S. American citizens during the first two decades of the 20th century caused large changes in both public and private life.

A suffragist works to win the vote for women, 1914. (Courtesy Library of Congress.)

## Responding to Information about the Rise of Large Industry and a Cry for Social Reform

How were your predictions? How about your classmates'? There was a lot happening in the United States at that time. When learning new information, it's often helpful to sort through it by looking at what is most important to you.

1. Make a list of the ideas from the reading that are most important to you personally. What do these ideas remind you of in your own life?

| Important Ideas | Things I Am Reminded of in My Life |
| --- | --- |
|  |  |
|  |  |
|  |  |
|  |  |

2. Choose one idea from your list and write a paragraph about it. Who or what does it remind you of in your personal life? Describe the person or event in detail.

## Understanding the Reading: Comprehension Check

Look at each topic and match it to the group that it is most closely related to in the reading by drawing a line between the two. The first one has been done for you.

immigration          alcohol drinkers
bribery              child laborers
agriculture          women
Mother Jones         factory owners
muckrakers           growing cities
prohibition          newspaper reporters
suffrage             farmers

Now that you have some basic knowledge of life in the United States at the beginning of the 20th century, let's apply it to something real from outside of the textbook.

### Talking about Work and Employment in Our Own Hometowns

The novel mentioned in the reading, *The Jungle*, is about a man and his job in a large factory. Since most of us have had a job before, we can use this knowledge along with what we have just learned to help us read and understand the passages from the novel that we are about to read. What was your first job? Did you like your first job? Before reading three paragraphs from Upton Sinclair's novel, conduct a mini-interview with a classmate and find out the following information about jobs.

> Your classmate's country, region, and hometown
> His/her first job
> Area's largest employer
> Importance of the company to the city or region
> Friends or relatives of your classmate who work there
> Treatment of workers by that company
> Classmate's personal experiences with that company, if any

It's always fun to find out new things about your classmates and their work experiences. What did you learn? Who had the most interesting job? Who liked their job the most? The least?

### *The Jungle:* Looking at a Novel by Upton Sinclair

*The Jungle* was written by Upton Sinclair and published in 1906. It is the story of an immigrant named Jurgis, who comes from Lithuania to seek fortune for himself and his family in the United States. Jurgis and his family settle in Chicago and begin to work in a meat factory. This story exposed the unsanitary conditions of the food industry in the United States, and it showed the hard lifestyle of the working class. It was a main cause of many reforms such as the *Pure Food and Drug Act* and laws to protect children from working in factories. Sinclair dedicated the book "To the workingmen of America."

Read these passages from *The Jungle*. The first one is from the beginning of the story when Jurgis and his family are new to America. Jurgis and Ona are engaged to be married. There are several aunts and uncles who came with him to the U.S. and brought their children. Some of the relatives pay rent to Jurgis. Jurgis and several adult members of the family have just found jobs at the factory in Packingtown—the stockyards of Chicago. Some unfamiliar words are explained for you in brackets [ ].

> Better luck than this could hardly be hoped for; there was only one of them left to seek a place. Jurgis was determined [*had decided*] that Teta Elzbieta should stay at home to keep house, and that Ona should help her. He would not have Ona working—he was not that sort of man, he said, and she was not that sort of woman. It would be a strange thing if a man like him could not support the family, with the help of the board [*rent money*] of Jonas and Marija. He would not even hear of letting the children go to work—there were schools here in America for children, Jurgis had heard, to which they could go for nothing. That the priest would object to these schools was something of which he had as yet no idea, and for the present his mind was made up that the children of Teta Elzbieta should have as fair a chance as any other children. The oldest of them, little Stanislovas, was but thirteen, and small for his age at that, and while the oldest son of Szedvillas was only twelve, and had worked for over a year at Jones', Jurgis would have it that Stanislovas should learn to speak English, and grow up to be a skilled man. (47–48)

This passage is from the middle of the story, after the family has found out that they were cheated when they bought a home. They cannot afford to pay the interest, so Ona pays a bribe and gets a job packing hams in tin cans at the factory. Then Jurgis sends his 14-year-old nephew Stanislovas to the city to look for work.

> And so, after little Stanislovas had stood gazing timidly [*scared*] about him for a few minutes, a man approached [*walked up to*] him and asked what he wanted, to which Stanislovas said "Job." Then the man said, "How old?" and Stanislovas answered "Sixtin." Once or twice every year a state inspector would come wandering through the packing plants, asking a child here and there how old he was; and so the packers were very careful to comply with [*follow*] the law, which cost them as much trouble as was now involved in taking the document [*birth certificate or proof of age*] from the boy, and glancing [*looking quickly and not carefully*] at it, and then sending it to the office to be filed away. Then he set someone else at a different job and showed the lad how to place a lard can every time the empty arm of the remorseless [*never stopping*] machine came to him; and so was decided the place in the universe of little Stanislovas, and his destiny to the end of his days. Hour after hour, day after day, year after

> year, it was fated that he should stand upon a certain square foot of floor from seven in the morning until noon, and again from half-past twelve till half-past five, making never a motion and thinking never a thought, save for [*except for*] the setting of the lard cans. In the summer the stench [*bad smell*] of the warm lard would be nauseating [*making somebody sick to the stomach*], and in the winter the cans would all but freeze to his naked little fingers in the unheated cellar. Half the year it would be dark as night when he went in to work, and dark as night again when he came out, and so he would never know what the sun looked like on weekdays [*Monday through Friday*]. And for this, at the end of the week, he would carry home three dollars to his family, being his pay at the rate of five cents per hour. . . ." (75–76)

The final passage is from the end of the novel. The people who were paying rent left, cutting the family's income by one-third. The grandfather and a child have died, and the whole family is fighting problems of various kinds. Most of the family members have lost their first jobs because of illness and have been forced to take lower-paying, more difficult jobs to survive.

> They were beaten; they had lost the game, they were swept aside. It was not less tragic because it was so sordid [*extremely base, dirty, and morally depressing*], because it had to do with wages and grocery bills and rents. They had dreamed of freedom; of a chance to look about them and learn something; to be decent and clean; to see their child grow up to be strong. And now it was all gone—it never would be! . . . Jurgis, being a man, had troubles of his own. There was another specter [*disturbing or haunting image; a ghost*] following him. He had never spoken of it, nor would he allow anyone else to speak of it—he had never acknowledged it [*admitted it to*] himself. Yet the battle with it took all manhood he had—and once or twice, alas, a little more. Jurgis had discovered drink [*alcohol*]. (138)

## Practicing Description

What do you think happens to Jurgis in the end? Tell another student your idea(s). The characters in the novel experience increased stress and their lives change a lot from the beginning of the story to the end. As their lives change, so do their attitudes. Based on what you've read here, make a list of as many adjectives as you can think of to describe Jurgis and his family at the beginning of the story, the middle of the story, and the end of the story.

| Beginning | Middle | End |
|-----------|--------|-----|
| *pleased* | | |
| *excited* | | |
| | | |
| | | |
| | | |
| | | |
| | | |

1. Adjectives and short phrases can be used to create a poem of sorts about the information you have. For example, this poem is about Packingtown and uses the letters of the name *Packingtown* as the first letters of adjectives or short phrases that describe information from the novel.

   **P** utrid
   **A** wful
   **C** old
   **K** illing animals
   **I** n a
   **N** ever-ending assembly line
   **G** ut shoveling Jurgis
   **T** ries to keep up
   **O** nly to be
   **W** orked to death
   **N** o more money; No more hope

   Use adjectives or phrases to make a similar poem with the first letters of words such as *factory, wages, monopoly, suffrage, alcohol*, etc. Use any vocabulary words from the list in the unit, or use any word you think is connected to the information in this unit.

2. When people change their attitude, it is often because of a realization. What realization do you think Jurgis and his family had about their situation? Describe in writing how you think Jurgis felt when he had that realization.

3. Did you ever have a realization about a personal situation? What was it? Write a narration about what happened. Describe

  the setting (where it happened, how things looked, smelled, sounded, etc.),
  what ideas led up to the realization,
  how the realization made you feel, and
  how things in your life are now different because of that realization.

## Speaking about Our Own Realizations: Culture Shock

Upton Sinclair wrote *The Jungle* to help people in the United States realize that the wealth of large industry was only an appearance—that many people worked in terrible conditions to make a few people wealthy. Although Sinclair's novel was intended mainly to expose the problems of capitalism, another major theme of *The Jungle* was the recognition by Jurgis and his family that life in the United States was not what they expected it to be.

It is often the same for people who travel to a foreign country, move to a new community, get married, have a child, go back to school, or start a new project. They imagine it to be a certain way, only to find out that it is not. If you recently moved to the U.S. to study English, or experienced any of these other things, you probably already know that.

This kind of negative realization is called **disillusionment.** Disillusionment is the second stage of "culture shock." It is a normal and expected part of living in a new culture. It is also common to experience this when undertaking a new project like going back to school, starting a new job, getting married, or buying a house. Look at the information below describing the stages and symptoms of culture shock.

| Stage | Symptoms |
|---|---|
| Honeymoon Stage | excitement, euphoria, feelings of control and confidence in the new country or situation |
| Disillusionment | frustration and anger, dislike of the new things which were once exciting, wanting to be with people from your own country or community, physical symptoms such as irritability or not sleeping |
| Culture Stress | some problems are solved and some are not, differences become less problematic, feelings of belonging to both the familiar and unfamiliar communities but not completely to either |
| Assimilation | acceptance of new culture or situation and self-confidence |

Are you experiencing or have you ever experienced any of these four stages of culture shock in any of your life situations? Make a list here.

Talk about culture shock with a classmate. Has your classmate experienced it or is he/she experiencing it now? What ideas do you have about coping with it or helping another person cope with it?

## Using Suggestion Phrases

You may be learning English with the future hope of living or studying in the United States or another English-speaking country. Many of you are probably new to the United States right now. Or maybe your parents experienced moving to this country and you have lived in the U.S. most or even all of your life. In any of these situations, the following activity will help you formulate some suggestions of things you can do to help yourself or to use your personal knowledge and experiences to help others with the disillusionment of culture shock. First, work with your instructor and classmates to rewrite these suggestion phrases in order from the least strong to the most strong. If you think two phrases are equal, write them next to each other.

| | Least Strong |
|---|---|
| It's a good idea to | |
| You must | |
| You should | |
| Let's | |
| Why don't you | |
| You ought to | |
| You might want to | |
| You could | |
| | Most Strong |

Talk about the order of your list with your classmates and instructor. (A note about sociolinguistic and appropriate English: In U.S. American culture, the phrase *you must* crosses the boundary line of suggestion. U.S. American English speakers understand *you must* as a soft command. *You must* should never be used when making a suggestion among equals or with a person of higher status. Please cross *you must* off your list of suggestion phrases.)

Practice with classmates by using the remaining suggestion phrases to suggest that they

get enough sleep,
eat nutritious food,
exercise regularly,
keep in contact with friends and family at home,
keep up on events at home via newspaper or Internet,
network with other foreign students,

join an international student club or other organization where they can meet native speakers,

keep an open mind and note new things that they like about the new country as well as the things that they dislike,

understand that learning to adapt to a new culture is a process and will not happen overnight,

understand that adapting to a new culture does not mean that they will lose their own.

What other suggestions do you have, based on your personal experience?

## College Drinking—What's So Special about a Fake ID?

Even though the government eliminated Prohibition, U.S. American attitudes about alcohol are still fairly conservative compared to those in many other countries. It is generally not considered socially acceptable for parents and children to drink together. Alcohol is taboo for many people. Some U.S. American states ban it from grocery stores and sell it only at state-controlled stores. Because the minimum age to buy or drink alcohol is 21, anti-alcohol campaigns are often aimed at teenagers. Many young people go to college at the age of 18 and are away from their parents for the first time. This new freedom and the forbidden nature of alcohol make drinking popular. Restaurants, bars, and stores ask young people to prove their age with identification before selling or serving them alcohol. In informal American English, this is called "being carded." When students make or buy an identification card with a false birthday in order to buy alcohol or go to bars, it is called a "fake ID".

A University of Arizona campaign to encourage responsible student drinking. (Courtesy University of Arizona Campus Health Service.)

## Fast Facts

- In 2002, 31% of students who participated in an alcohol use survey can be considered alcohol abusers. 6% were considered to be dependent on alcohol.

- Alcohol abuse experts cite drinking as the #1 health risk for college students, with a 1999 Harvard study showing that 44% "binge drink" (consume five or more drinks at a time for men and four or more at a time for women).

- Studies published in the *New England Journal of Medicine* and the *Journal of the American Medical Association* report that one or two drinks per day reduces the risk of some kinds of stroke by anywhere from 20 to 50%.

- Research conducted by Dr. Scott Schwarzwelder and his lab group at Duke University found that alcohol caused more learning and memory problems for 21–24 year-old students than it did for those aged 25–29.

- Numerous medical studies in recent years have confirmed that moderate drinking reduces the risk of heart disease and heart attack.

**Positive Aspects of Drinking Alcohol**
Find and read a newspaper, magazine, or Internet article on a positive aspect of alcohol consumption. Summarize it in your own words.

**Negative Aspects of Drinking Alcohol**
Find and read a newspaper, magazine, or Internet article on a negative aspect of alcohol consumption. Summarize it in your own words.

**My Personal Conclusion(s) about College Drinking in the United States**

## Putting It All Together

You have just taken a whirlwind tour of life in the U.S. at the turn of the 20th century and today. That is a lot to deal with all at once, so now is the time to step back and think about what you have learned in this unit. First, take some quiet time to write down your ideas about these questions. Then, in groups of three, talk about the following questions and/or others you may have. After you have discussed your ideas as a group, you should present them to the whole class.

1. What surprised me most about the United States in the early part of the 20th century?

2. What does this information help me to understand about modern U.S. American life?

3. How does knowing this information change my mind about U.S. American values and attitudes?

4. Can I learn something from the lessons the U.S. learned from the Prohibition and social reform era? Can my community learn something from this information?

5. What will I tell somebody now if he or she asks me about the role of alcohol in the United States today?

6. What kinds of positive changes can be made regarding social reform for workers in various countries? In my own community?

# 2 The U.S. between World Wars

## The Roaring Twenties, Black Tuesday, and Beyond

Representative T. S. McMillan of Charleston, S.C., with flappers who are doing the Charleston during the 1920s. (Photo by National Photo Co., Courtesy Library of Congress.)

## Net Surfers

See what information you can find by searching for the following names, words, and phrases on the World Wide Web.

| | |
|---|---|
| All about jazz | Isolationism |
| Civilian Conservation Corps | The Jazz Age page |
| Documenting America | Jazz biographies |
| Dust bowl history | The 1920s experience |
| GORP U.S. National Parks and Preserves | Prohibition and the Roaring Twenties |
| The history of jazz music | Social Security Administration |

## *Presidential Suite*

Woodrow Wilson (D) 1913–21
Warren G. Harding (R) 1921–23
Calvin Coolidge (R) 1923–29
Herbert C. Hoover (R) 1929–33
Franklin Delano Roosevelt (D) 1933–45

## *On TV*

*The Waltons*

## *Music Box*

"Are You Makin' Any Money?" - Chick Bullock and His Levee Loungers (1933)
"Brother, Can You Spare a Dime?" - Rudy Vallee (1932)
"Gloomy Sunday" - Billie Holiday (1941)
"Happy Days Are Here Again" - Casa Loma Orchestra (1929)
"Headin' For Better Times" - Ted Lewis and His Band (1931)
"It Don't Mean a Thing (If It Ain't Got That Swing)" - Duke Ellington and His Orchestra (1932)
"There's a New Day Comin'" - Ted Lewis and His Band (1933)
"We Sure Got Hard Times Now" - Barbecue Bob (1930)

## *At the Movies*

*The Grapes of Wrath* (adapted from a novel)
*Of Mice and Men* (adapted from a novel)

## Preparing to Read about the Roaring Twenties, Black Tuesday, and Beyond

Many changes occurred during the first two decades of the twentieth century for the United States. Most of that change was for the better, but in this unit the focus is on change from positive to negative. This isn't uncommon: a country's ride through history is full of ups and downs. In this unit, you will reflect on your own experiences through an interview activity. Take notes on what your classmate says in the space provided. Get comfortable with a classmate, set aside your grammar worries, and do your best to find out information

about good times
    the places where your classmate and his/her friends go to have a good time
    the attitude of his/her parents or older generations about those places/activities
    the public attitude toward those places/activities

about war
    the wars that the U.S. or your classmate's country has been involved in
    the public acceptance of war in his/her community
    the attitude of your classmate toward war

about poverty
    the situation of poor people in your classmate's community
    the government's efforts to deal with it
    the public attitude toward poor people

Share what you learned in your interview with your classmates and your instructor. As always, it is okay to keep personal information confidential if you choose to.

## Learning New Vocabulary about the U.S. between World Wars

**advocate (n)** a supporter; somebody who promotes something

**conservation (n)** keeping something nice or protected/preserved

**dissatisfaction (n)** a state of unhappiness over something

**drought (n)** an extended period without rain in which no crops can grow

**flapper (n)** name for a modern woman in the 1920s

**Great Depression (n)** a time of economic problems in the U.S. between 1929–1941

**isolationism (n)** belief in only wanting to deal with one's own existence

**leadership (n)** the ability to lead or be in charge of something

**poverty (n)** the state of not having enough money; being poor

**renaissance (n)** a rebirth

**salary (n)** money earned for work; based on yearly earnings

**self-confidence (n)** strong belief in oneself

**topsoil (n)** the top layer of soil rich in nutrients and good for plants

**wealth (n)** the state of having a lot of money

**to approve (v)** to think well of; to give permission for something

**to commit (v)** to promise focus and effort to one thing

**to cope (v)** to deal with; to handle

**to criticize (v)** to speak poorly of; to disapprove

**to sweep (v)** to take over or spread from one area to another

**to wipe out (v)** to completely destroy; to no longer exist

**especially (adv)** to a large degree

Even though all of the new words are important, the words we will discuss at length in the next activity are especially necessary to understanding some major attitudes in the United States between World War I and World War II. It helps to ask yourself questions about all of the new vocabulary when you have some extra time at home.

## Talking about New Words and Ideas

1. When a country makes an effort to preserve its natural resources, it is referred to as an act of **conservation.** The U.S. has a long tradition of setting aside places of natural beauty and protecting them from development. The United States' first national park, Yellowstone, was set aside in 1879.

   A.  What effects of conservation do you see today in U.S. society?
   B.  Do you think this trend will continue in the future, or do you see it declining?
   C.  How do you think people in other countries view U.S. conservation efforts?
   D.  What do you think other countries should do to promote conservation efforts?
   E.  List some words that are related to **conservation** in your mind.

Old Faithful erupts at Yellowstone National Park.

2. When a country does not want to get involved in the problems of other countries and instead prefers to concentrate on internal issues, it is said to be in a phase of **isolationism.** The United States has gone through various stages of isolationism, even though many believe that the United States acts as the "police officer to the world."

   A. Can you think of a specific crisis that the United States chose not to be involved in?
   B. Why do you think the United States chose not to get involved?
   C. What countries today have an isolationist mentality?
   D. Is a country's isolationist mentality an advantage or a disadvantage?
   E. Is it possible for one country to choose only to deal with its own problems in a global society?
   F. List some words that are related to **isolationism** in your mind.

3. When something experiences a rebirth in society, it is said to be undergoing a **renaissance.** For example, in the United States today, people talk of an urban renaissance, meaning that the large cities are being reborn after a long period of decay. Certain kinds of literature, music, or art also experience a renaissance at various time periods. For example, swing music and dancing from the 1920s is now popular among younger U.S. Americans.

   A. Is there something in your community that is experiencing a renaissance? If so, what?
   B. Why do you think old-fashioned things become popular again with younger generations?
   C. List some words that are related to **renaissance** in your mind.

4. When someone is a strong supporter of something, we say that he or she is an **advocate.** If you look closely at the word *advocate*, you will notice that it contains the stem *voc*, which is also a root of *voice* and *vocal.* So, we can know that the word *advocate* has to do with somebody who uses his/her voice or speaks up for something and promotes it publicly.

   A. Are you an advocate for something? If so, what?
   B. How do you promote it?

C.  What is the result of your being an advocate for something? Has your effort been successful?

D.  List some words that are related to **advocate** in your mind.

5.  When someone takes the responsibility of being in charge of something, we say that he or she has assumed a **leadership** role.

A.  Have you ever taken a leadership role in an activity or in your community?

B.  Do you like or dislike being a leader? For what reason(s)?

C.  How acceptable is it for women to take leadership positions in your community?

D.  List some words that are related to **leadership** in your mind.

## Making Predictions about the Reading

Making predictions about a reading is beneficial to language learning. So, in pairs or in a small group, review the discussion you had with your classmates about good times, war, and poverty and the new words you learned. Based on this discussion, make a list of five things you think will be in the next reading selection.

1.

2.

3.

4.

5.

Compare your list with the lists of two other students in your class. What ideas are similar? Which are different? Are there any ideas from your classmates that make you think you might like to change your ideas? If so, write them down here.

## Reading about the U.S. between World Wars

In the middle of a period of internal progress, the United States found itself involved in World War I. Although the war lasted from 1914 to 1918, the United States became involved in 1917. President Woodrow Wilson, an **advocate** of peace and neutrality, wanted to keep the U.S. out of the war, but he asked Congress to declare war on Germany in 1917 as the result of continued German attacks on U.S. and British merchant ships and the sinking of a British passenger ship, the *Lusitania.* Once the war ended a year later, the U.S. returned its attention to a booming economy and growing **self-confidence** as a nation, **committing** itself to **isolationism** and attention to its own existence.

The 1920s were known as the Roaring Twenties. During these ten years, the nation's **wealth** doubled, and the **salary** of the average worker grew 10% higher. The dollar became strong, and the New York stock market soared. Theater, literature, and art experienced a **renaissance,** and movies

President Wilson addresses Congress regarding U.S. involvement in World War I, February 3, 1917. (Courtesy DoD Visual Information Record Center.)

The great jazz musician Duke Ellington. (Courtesy DoD Visual Information Record Center.)

were the newest rage. Jazz, a new form of music with its birthplace in New Orleans, **swept** the country with artists such as Duke Ellington and Louis Armstrong playing the wild music that the young loved despite their parents' **dissatisfaction.** Women **especially,** enjoying the new confidence gained from their **leadership** in reform movements and voting rights, were progressive during this time. The short "bobbed" hair, shorter skirts (no longer floor-length), and cigarette smoking of these **flappers** were viewed as immoral.

This all came to an end when the stock market crashed on October 24, 1929, known as Black Tuesday. Many people's bank savings were **wiped out** overnight. The economic crisis was not only on Wall Street, however, as farms and businesses went down and unemployment went up. In addition to these problems, parts of the Midwest and the Southwest were also experiencing a severe **drought** that made it impossible to grow crops. Much of the **topsoil** dried, cracked, and was blown away in a natural event, that came to be called the Dust Bowl. Thus, in the 1930s, up to one-quarter of U.S.

A young man copes with the Great Depression. (Courtesy Library of Congress.)

Americans found themselves unemployed and **coping** with an economic crisis known as the Great Depression. **Poverty** in the United States resulted in the appearance of cardboard and wood scrap houses outside of cities. Called Hoovervilles, they were named after the current president, Herbert Hoover. In the cities, thousands stood in line daily for a meal of soup and bread.

Noting that he saw one-third of a nation in poverty and promising U.S. Americans a "New Deal," Franklin D. Roosevelt (FDR) was elected president in 1932. Roosevelt set to work, and within the first 100 days of his presidency, Congress had **approved** a number of emergency projects to help U.S. citizens **cope** with the Depression. One of the most important was the Works Progress Administration (WPA), a plan to employ millions of people

WPA hiking trail project, Tucson, Arizona.

while improving roads, dams, sidewalks, and schools. In addition, many forest **conservation** projects, hiking trails, and national park beautification projects came about because of the Civilian Conservation Corps (CCC). Some **criticized** this program, thinking it was socialist; the program was even questioned by the Supreme Court. Despite these problems, this "alphabet soup" of programs continued until World War II. The United States entered the war in 1941, but only after the Japanese bombed the U.S. naval base at Pearl Harbor (in Hawaii, which was not yet a U.S. state).

## Responding to Information about the Roaring Twenties, Black Tuesday, and Beyond

How were your predictions? How were your classmates' predictions?

1. Make a summary of the main ideas from the reading, what they remind you of personally, and what connection you make between them and what you know about U.S. American life.

| Main Ideas | Reminds Me Personally of | Connection to U.S. American Life |
|---|---|---|
|  |  |  |
|  |  |  |
|  |  |  |
|  |  |  |

2. Choose what you think is the most important main idea from your list and write a paragraph about it. Describe how it is important to you personally. Describe how you connect it to your knowledge of U.S. American life or U.S. American citizens.

## Understanding the Reading: Comprehension Check

This comprehension check is a summary/paraphrase of the reading with some incorrect words. This is a little reading test, so without giving in to the temptation to look back at the text, use your new understanding and knowledge to circle the best word for the sentence.

Even though the United States did not want to, it became involved in World War I because of German attacks on British and American (war/passenger) ships. After the war, the United States decided to focus on (itself/other countries). The 1920s were a (depressing/wild) time. People had a lot of (fun/problems). There were new (dances, movies, and music/sports, TV shows, and radios) to entertain people. Women became more (progressive/conservative). Older people (celebrated/rejected) the new ways. When the stock market crashed, people (panicked/rejoiced) because they were (rich/destroyed). The Great Depression caused (unemployment and homelessness/an economic boom and security). President Franklin Delano Roosevelt promised to (help Americans/fight the Germans). The New Deal gave U.S. Americans (problems and fear/jobs and hope). Many people thought the New Deal was (capitalist/socialist). In the end, it (hurt/helped) many people.

Check your answers with your classmates and instructor. If you missed several, go back and read the text again and try to focus on reading more carefully. Once you have understood the reading text completely, the fun can begin as you use your knowledge of Roosevelt's New Deal and apply it to something outside of the textbook.

## Viewing WPA Photography

During the Great Depression, President Franklin Delano Roosevelt stated that one-third of the nation was living in poverty. His Works Progress Administration (WPA) was designed to put as many people to work as possible. Projects were designed to be large and/or elaborate so that as many crafts- and tradespeople as possible could work on them. While many were put to work constructing large buildings, dams, and projects, others set to work on beautification efforts such as sculptures, murals, and paintings. Some people felt that these projects were a waste of time, but if you look carefully when you visit the United States, you will find that many still exist, beautifying public places.

A large group of artists including playwrights, painters, musicians, writers, and photographers was also put to work creating plays and songs or writing and documenting on film the life histories of the U.S. American population. One such project, entitled "One Third of a Nation" by photographers Arnold Eagle and David Robbins, documented the Great Depression via photography. Others feature the photographs of Dorothea Lange, a well-known Depression era photographer. Lange described taking her photos of a migrant mother:

I saw and approached the hungry and desperate mother, as if drawn by a magnet. I do not remember how I explained my presence or my camera to her, but I do remember she asked me no questions. I made five exposures, working closer and closer from the same direction. I did not ask her name or her history. She told me her age, that she was thirty-two. She said that they had been living on frozen vegetables from the surrounding fields, and birds that the children killed. She had just sold the tires from her car to buy food.

A migrant mother. (Courtesy Library of Congress.)

A woman and her children face the Great Depression. (Courtesy Library of Congress.)

*Mother and Boy at Table.* Slum conditions in the congested East Side and Charles districts of New York City are recorded in a group "One Third of a Nation," 1938. (WPA Photo. Courtesy U.S. National Archives and Records Administration.).

Look at the three photos and answer the questions.

| | Migrant Mother | Woman and Children | Mother and Boy at Table |
|---|---|---|---|
| What is happening in the photograph? | | | |
| What time period does it seem to be? | | | |
| What is the mood of the people? | | | |
| What do the people do for a living? | | | |
| How are the people related to each other? | | | |
| What is similar in all of the photos? | | | |
| What is different in each of the photos? | | | |
| What is the photographer's message? | | | |

Use the answers to these questions and your creativity to narrate a story about the people in the photos. You may use the photos in any sequence you wish, but make sure that each photograph illustrates part of your story. Be as creative as you like.

## Using Backchanneling Strategies to Show Our Own Interest in Speaker Narratives

When native speakers of U.S. American English want to show interest in a narrative or other information given by another speaker, they often use a strategy called *backchanneling*. This is a kind of verbal and nonverbal feedback that shows our interest and emotions, telling the speaker that we are listening and interested in hearing him/her continue. U.S. American English speakers rely on this feedback, and if they don't get it, they may stop communicating. So, if you as a nonnative speaker remain completely silent, you may confuse the native speaker and hinder communication. But don't overdo it either! A good rule of thumb is a nod or verbal acknowledgment such as *mmmm* or *uh-huh* for every three or four sentences spoken. Look at this list of words and phrases commonly used for backchanneling and their functions.

| Word or Phrase | Function |
| --- | --- |
| Uh-huh.<br>Mmmmm.<br>(Nodding head up and down.) | Signal listening and the listener's willingness to have the speaker continue without interruption. |
| I see.<br>Ahhhh.<br>And then? | Signal listening for content and the wish for more information. |
| Oh?<br>Oh, really?<br>Oh, yeah?<br>Wow! | Signal mild surprise and the wish for the speaker to continue giving information. Can also signal a little doubt, usually with facial expressions such as wrinkled eyebrows. |

| Word or Phrase | Function |
|---|---|
| Ah-hah! | Signals a wished-for or key piece of information. |
| That's nice. | Signals noncommittal listening to content. Is sometimes used sarcastically to indicate boredom. |
| Sure. | Signals general agreement with the speaker's viewpoints and a supportive stance. |
| No way! | Signals disagreement. Can also signal strong surprise but general agreement with speaker's viewpoint in younger circles. |
| No.<br>Uh-uh. | Signal disagreement. |
| All right. | Signals agreement, usually about plans. In younger circles, can signal approval (stress on *right*). |
| Sounds great! | Signals strong agreement, usually about plans. |
| Awwww. | Signals mild dismay or sympathy. |
| Gee, I don't know.<br>Hmmm. | Signal inability to respond to information but not disagreement. |
| Oh, sorry.<br>Sorry, go on.<br>Sorry, you were saying? | Signals improper interruption on the listener's part and the listener's wish to apologize and let the speaker continue. |

Work in groups of three. One person is the storyteller, one person is the listener, and one person is the observer. The storyteller tells the listener the story he/she wrote about the photos. The listener practices using appropriate backchanneling strategies. The observer should not speak at all, but should note the backchanneling phrases used and whether they were effective. The observer shares his/her notes with the storyteller and listener, and the group discusses the experience. Continue until each person in the group has had a turn to be the storyteller, the listener, and the observer.

## Understanding More about Conservation: Touring the National Park System

The National Park Service was created on August 25, 1916, by President Woodrow Wilson to protect the 40 national parks that already existed. Through the years, another 15 were added, bringing today's total to 55. In addition to the 55 national parks, there are many national monuments, preserves, battlefields, recreation areas, and historic sites, which make a total of 390 in the national system. Each state also has a similar system of state parks, monuments, and the like. The U.S. state with the most national parks is Utah, with a total of five: Arches, Bryce Canyon, Canyonlands, Capitol Reef, and Zion.

A current list of national parks in the United States follows:

| | | |
|---|---|---|
| Acadia | Grand Canyon | North Cascades |
| Arches | Grand Teton | Olympic |
| Badlands | Great Basin | Petrified Forest |
| Big Bend | Great Smokey Mountains | Redwood |
| Biscayne | Guadalupe Mountains | Rocky Mountain |
| Black Canyon | Haleakala | Saguaro |
| Bryce Canyon | Hawaii Volcanoes | Samoa |
| Canyonlands | Hot Springs | Sequoia |
| Capitol Reef | Isle Royale | Shenandoah |
| Carlsbad Caverns | Joshua Tree | Theodore Roosevelt |
| Channel Islands | Katmai | Virgin Islands |
| Crater Lake | Kenai Fjords | Voyageurs |
| Death Valley | Kings Canyon | Wind Cave |
| Denali | Kobuk Valley | Wrangell–St. Elisa |
| Dry Tortugas | Lake Clark | Yellowstone |
| Everglades | Lassen Volcanic | Yosemite |
| Gates of the Arctic | Mammoth Cave | Zion |
| Glacier | Mesa Verde | |
| Glacier Bay | Mount Rainier | |

The sun sets over Saguaro National Park.

Visitors stand under one of the many massive arches at Arches National Park.

The magnificent Grand Canyon

Choose a national park, and look it up in an encyclopedia in the library or on the Internet. Be sure to type the words *national park* after the name if you choose to use the Internet. Prepare a five- to ten-minute presentation about the park for your class. Include the following information for your classmates:

- In which U.S. state is the national park located?
- How old is it?
- When is the best time to visit?
- What are the highlights of the national park?
- What cities is the park close to?
- What is the best way to get there?

## The Social Security Debate—Who Will Pay for the Young When They Get Old?

The Social Security Act was passed by Congress in 1935. It gives a pension to U.S. Americans over the age of 65. It is paid for by a deduction from employee wages that is matched by employers. The idea behind Social Security is that people pay into it when they are young and employed and then get money back when they are older and retired. Because of the large number of people in the "baby boom" generation (babies born in the decades after World War II) who will be retiring in the next few years, many fear that the money for the system will be depleted, leaving the current college-aged generation of taxpayers and those who follow with nothing for their retirement. Others fear that privatizing the system by allowing workers to invest Social Security taxes in the stock market is too risky. Look at these pieces of information. What conclusions can you make about Social Security?

## Fast Facts

- It is predicted that by the year 2015, 77 million retired "baby boomers" will be drawing more from Social Security than younger workers are putting in.

- Six out of every ten U.S. Americans polled prior to the 2000 presidential election thought privatizing Social Security was a good idea.

- By 2039, Social Security is projected to require either benefit cuts of up to 1/3 to recipients or a 50% increase on taxes workers pay into it.

- Legislation was passed by Congress in 2000 to remove the benefits penalty for senior citizens aged 65–69 who choose to remain employed in the workforce.

**Positive Aspects of Social Security Reform**
Find and read a newspaper, magazine, or Internet article on a positive aspect of Social Security reform. Summarize it in your own words.

**Negative Aspects of Social Security Reform**
Find and read a newspaper, magazine, or Internet article on a negative aspect of Social Security reform. Summarize it in your own words.

**My Personal Conclusion(s) about Social Security in the United States**

## Putting It All Together

With each unit, you will learn more and more new information about U.S. culture and history. It is important to take some time to process new information. Step back and think about all the new information you learned in this unit. First, take some time to reflect and write your ideas about these questions. Then, in groups of three, talk about the following questions and/or others you may have. After you have discussed your ideas as a group, present them to the whole class.

1. What surprised me most about the Roaring Twenties? About the Great Depression?

2. What does this information help me to understand about modern U.S. American life?

3. How does knowing this information change my mind about U.S. American values and attitudes?

4. Can people in other countries learn something from the lessons the United States took from the Roaring Twenties and the Great Depression? If so, what?

5. What will I tell people now if they ask me about the U.S. between World War I and World War II?

6. What kinds of positive changes can other countries make regarding conservation or providing for people's retirement needs?

# 3 The U.S. after World War II

## Consumer Culture, Suburbia, and the Baby Boom

Teens learn the latest rock 'n' roll dance moves, 1953. (Photo by Fred Palumbo. Courtesy Library of Congress.)

## Net Surfers

See what information you can find by searching for the following names, words, and phrases on the World Wide Web.

All consuming passion: waking up from the American Dream

Andy Warhol reference page

Antique Hollywood postcards

The baby boom at mid-decade

Credit cards and college students

Credit card companies

Credit counseling

Elvis-Presley.com

Graceland

Greg Knight's patio culture

LIFE baby boom home page

Pop art index

Sun Studio, birthplace of rock 'n' roll

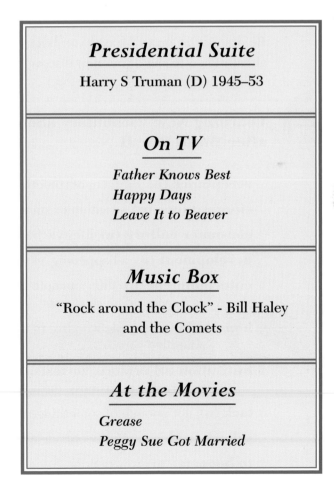

## *Presidential Suite*

Harry S Truman (D) 1945–53

## *On TV*

*Father Knows Best*
*Happy Days*
*Leave It to Beaver*

## *Music Box*

"Rock around the Clock" - Bill Haley and the Comets

## *At the Movies*

*Grease*
*Peggy Sue Got Married*

## Preparing to Read about Consumer Culture, Suburbia, and the Baby Boom

This unit addresses economy and capitalism after World War II. This unit also begins with an interview. Team up with a classmate and find out:

about consuming
> the things your classmate spends his/her extra money on
> the type of advertising he/she likes and dislikes
> the reaction of consumers in his/her community to advertising

about economies
> the economy in his/her community
> the way your classmate feels about that economic system
> the way people in his/her community live because of that economic system

Before moving on to the new vocabulary words for the unit, use the words you already know to share your new discoveries in a small or large group discussion.

## Learning New Vocabulary about the U.S. after World War II

**acceptance (n)** thinking of something as correct, right, or okay

**circumstance (n)** situation or surroundings

**consumer culture (n)** lifestyle based on buying and using products

**development (n)** a happening, especially one with new results

**entertainment (n)** things people do for fun in their free time, such as movies or sports events

**household (n)** people who live in the same house or apartment, often a family

**institution (n)** organization that makes up a society such as a school, government, business, etc.

**lack (n)** not enough of something (most often used as a verb)

**suburb (n)** a community outside a city with many houses and schools

**to boom (v)** to grow rapidly

**to combine (v)** to put two or more things together to form something new

**to influence (v)** to change in indirect ways

**eager (adj)** very interested in something and wanting to do it quickly

**ideological (adj)** based on ideas or beliefs

**immoral (adj)** not meeting standards of what is good or right in society

**permanent (adj)** lasting forever, not temporary

**scarce (adj)** little or not enough of

**willing (adj)** wanting to do something without being forced to

## Talking about New Words and Ideas

Use your understanding of the new vocabulary words to discuss the following questions with a partner or in a group.

1. In the United States, the belief in capitalism and democracy is the **ideological** foundation of the government and daily life for most people. Many people will tell you that these beliefs are worth fighting for and that they guarantee freedoms for U.S. American citizens. Others will tell you that they have grown too large and are hurting people who cannot compete against big businesses and the amount of money needed to participate in politics. Ideological foundations that form a basis for people's lives include economic ideologies, political ideologies, religious ideologies, and gender ideologies, to name a few.

   A. What ideological foundation(s) has/have influenced your life the most?

   B. Do most people in your community believe in this/these ideologies?

   C. How do people in your community behave based on these ideologies?

   D. Do you think any ideology in your life or the lives of those around you needs to change?

   E. How do you think people in the U.S. behave based on their ideologies?

   F. Do you think the ideology in the U.S. needs to change?

   G. List some words that are related to **ideology** in your mind.

2. Anything that does not conform to a society's agreed-upon moral principles is said to be **immoral** by the majority. These moral principles often have their roots in a country's history. For example, some of the early settlers of the United States were a religious group called the Puritans. They had very strict moral codes regarding sexuality. This strict value system still influences many U.S. Americans' public opinions about sexuality today, although this is being challenged more and more.

   A.  What is considered to be immoral by the majority in your community?
   B.  Do most people in your community agree with this in their private lives?
   C.  Do you think that some things that your grandparents thought were immoral are okay today? An example?
   D.  How do you view U.S. American citizens in terms of morality?
   E.  Do you think the idea of what is immoral is changing or will change in the U.S.? In your community?
   F.  List some words that are related to **immoral** in your mind.

3. When people move out of the cities into housing communities just outside of the cities, they are said to be moving to the **suburbs.** Many inner cities in the U.S. have decayed as businesses and people moved away from the city to the suburbs. One example of the result of such movement is a large difference in the quality of schools. Since people who live in the suburbs tend to earn more money than people who live in cities, suburban schools are usually much better off than inner city schools. This is mostly because money for schools comes from property taxes in school districts and property values are higher in the suburbs than in the cities, so more tax money is available for schools there.

   A.  Do most of the people you know live in cities, suburbs, or rural areas?
   B.  Do you notice differences in income between people who live in cities, suburbs, and rural areas?
   C.  What do you think of the U.S. tendency to move to the suburbs?
   D.  What are the benefits of such a move for U.S. citizens? Drawbacks?
   E.  List some words that are related to **suburbs** in your mind.

4. When something increases rapidly, U.S. Americans say that there was a **boom.** For example, since the 1980s there has been a population boom in the Southwest of the United States. Many people moved from the North to the Southwest because of the warmer weather and businesses that moved their offices there. There can also be a boom created by an abundance of a particular product; an oil boom in Texas or a copper boom in Arizona are examples of this. We might speak of a population boom on a global scale, as the number of people in the world increases rapidly.

A. Has your geographic region ever experienced a boom in something? What?

B. What was the effect of this boom on your community? Your family? You?

C. List some words that are related to **boom** in your mind.

## Making Predictions about the Reading

Work in a small group of three students to make predictions about the reading. Without looking ahead to the reading, review together the main ideas you discussed and the new ideas you learned about from the new vocabulary words. Then agree on five ideas you expect to be introduced in the reading based on the information you have already. Your whole group must agree before you write the ideas down.

1.

2.

3.

4.

5.

## Reading about the U.S. after World War II

At midcentury, the two main results from the United States' participation in World War II were an expanded consumer culture based on newly found spending power and the birth of the United States as a "superpower" involved in an **ideological** cold war with the Soviet Union. Both of these **developments influenced** the way U.S. citizens think of themselves and the world. Since the middle of the twentieth century, Americans have viewed themselves as part of a rich and powerful nation where, because of capitalism and democracy, anyone who is **willing** to work hard can make it to the top regardless of the **circumstances** into which he or she was born. Although this "American Dream" has been a strong principle for U.S. citizens since the United States was formed in the late 1700s, it was the **consumer culture** and the fight for democracy that lent power to the American Dream for many citizens.

Following the Great Depression, the production needs for fighting World War II caused industry in the U.S. to **boom.** Factories were producing at full

Famous World War II poster featuring "Rosie the Riveter." Poster by J. Howard Miller. (Courtesy DoD Visual Information Record Center.)

speed, and many married women whose husbands were overseas went to work for the first time, learning new skills, earning money, and gaining new confidence. Because of the **lack** of money in most U.S. **households** during the Great Depression, followed by **scarce** supplies during World War II, many U.S. citizens were able and **eager** to spend money after the war. They bought homes in the new and growing **suburbs** and large appliances to put in them such as refrigerators, washers, and dryers. They purchased automobiles to drive to work in the city. They had babies in record numbers, creating a baby boom generation, referring to those children born in the U.S. between 1946–64, resulting in the growth of the middle class.

In addition, what has come to be called the **entertainment** industry began to play a more important role. Some of the products that are often associated with the rise of this industry include Hollywood, films, television, frozen "TV dinners," and McDonald's, all of which were successful because

Marilyn Monroe appears with the U.S.O. show "Anything Goes," 1954. (Courtesy DoD Visual Information Record Center.)

Teenage girls add to graffiti on an Elvis movie poster, 1956. (Photo by Phil Stanziola. Courtesy Library of Congress.)

middle class Americans had extra money to spend. The history of music was also changed at this time by a man born into a poor family in Tupelo, Mississippi: Elvis Presley. Up until that time, many African Americans in the United States listened to rhythm and blues or jazz music, whereas whites primarily listened to bluegrass, country, and big bands. Elvis **combined** these kinds of music for a new sound that became known as rock 'n' roll.

Many older people rejected Presley and his new music, thinking that it was **immoral.** His dance moves were said to be too sexual for Elvis to be shown below the waist on television. However, teenagers loved him and his music. Their **acceptance** of his new style showed early approval of a new sexual freedom that later exploded in the 1960s, **permanently** changing values and **institutions** in the United States.

## Responding to Information about Consumer Culture, Suburbia, and the Baby Boom

When we understand what we read, we often are able to form a picture or an image of what we are reading in our minds. As you were reading, did you visualize some of the ideas that you read about? Expressing those images helps us to remember the things we read. This is my response to the reading.

What is your response to the information in the reading? Use the space below to express your reaction to the reading in any way you choose.

## Understanding the Reading: Comprehension Check

This comprehension check is a true/false test. True/false is a popular way of testing at large, public educational institutions in the United States because it is easy to score by computer. Some beginning general education courses can have as many as 500 students, so professors and instructors tend to look for ways to save time on grading. Have you ever seen one of these tests before? Have you heard of them? Almost every U.S. American student has taken a true/false test at some time. The trick to a true/false statement is that if any part of the statement is not true, then the answer is False. Also, words like *always, every, only,* and *all* are usually a good clue that the answer is False. Try this popular U.S. American testing technique and see how you do. Circle True or False for each statement below.

1. The only changes in the lives of U.S. citizens after World War II were access to more spending money and living in a country that was a superpower.  True  False

2. The American Dream became a new idea after World War II.  True  False

3. With their extra money, people bought cars, homes, and appliances.  True  False

4. The middle class in the United States became smaller after World War II.  True  False

5. The entertainment industry fueled Hollywood, McDonald's, and TV dinners.  True  False

6. Everybody loved Elvis Presley's new kind of music.  True  False

7. Rock 'n' roll contributed to public value changes in the U.S. after World War II.  True  False

What did you think about this kind of test? Was it tricky? True/false is designed to quickly weed out students who know the information from students who don't. It's OK if you got some of the questions wrong, as this is probably the first time you've seen a test like this. This is part of learning about culture too. Let's turn back to the topic of consumer culture. Andy Warhol was a famous artist who didn't like what he saw during the time of rising consumer culture, and he expressed his criticism through his art.

## Looking at Consumer Culture: Andy Warhol's Pop Art

Andy Warhola was born in 1928 in Pittsburgh, Pennsylvania, the son of Czech immigrants. His father died when Andy was 14, so he worked his way through art school at the Carnegie Institute of Technology on a scholarship and had a job at a dairy store creating window displays. He Americanized his name after he moved to New York; his goal was to become famous. He did commercial art for advertisers and window displays for a few years until pop art spread from Britain to New York in the late 1950s.

The goal of pop art was to satirize consumer culture. With the boom in the U.S. American economy and the extra purchasing power of the people, companies began to increase efforts to mass-market products to a mass consumer audience. Andy Warhol's work became a famous commentary on U.S. American society. His portrayal of repetition was a satire on consumers' buying habits. When it came to his work, nothing was sacred. Warhol depicted objects such as Campbell's soup cans, Coke bottles, Brillo soap pad boxes, shoes, and dollar bills. He also portrayed famous people, such as Marilyn Monroe, Elvis Presley, and Jackie Kennedy.

Some examples of Andy Warhol's work can be viewed on the Web. Conduct a search on Andy Warhol to find a site that inlcudes some of Warhol's paintings. Look at three different paintings by Andy Warhol. Think about them and then answer the following questions. There are no right or wrong answers.

| | What is Warhol's main message to the audience? | What specific aspect of society is being criticized? | Is the criticism harsh and direct or more soft and indirect? |
|---|---|---|---|
| Painting One | | | |
| Painting Two | | | |
| Painting Three | | | |

## Using Hedging Techniques to Express Our Own Critical Observations

Native speakers of U.S. American English are generally a little less direct about expressing critical observations than in many other cultures. Often, they are surprised and sometimes offended at the directness of nonnative speakers. While it is acceptable in U.S. American society to make positive and negative observations—and is even insisted upon in U.S. American classroom settings when discussing ideas and class readings—it is accomplished appropriately by a technique called *hedging*. Hedging makes observations less direct by softening the blow with a positive observation that balances out the negative. Some good hedging words to start out with are:

Although . . .
Even though . . .
Though . . .
While . . .

You can see what kind of effect using these words has on critical observations when you compare these two sentences about the Andy Warhol paintings:

Positive Observation: *The subject is interesting.*
Critical Observation: *The colors in the painting are annoying.*
Hedged Critical Observation: *Although the subject is interesting, the colors in the painting are annoying.*

Does this technique soften the negative observations and make them seem more polite?

Here are some examples of how the other hedging words look in a sentence:

**Even though** *the subject is interesting, the colors in the painting are annoying.*
**Though** *the subject is interesting, the colors in the painting are annoying.*
**While** *the subject is interesting, the colors in the painting are annoying.*

Make a list of five positive and five negative observations about the three pieces of Andy Warhol work you chose from the Web site.

| Positive Observations | Negative Observations |
| --- | --- |
| Example: *The subject is interesting.* | Example: *The colors are annoying.* |
| 1. | 1. |
| 2. | 2. |
| 3. | 3. |
| 4. | 4. |
| 5. | 5. |

Now place one of the hedging words or phrases before any one of the positive observations, add a comma, and then state one of the negative observations.

Example: **Although** the subject is interesting, the colors are annoying.

1.
2.
3.
4.
5.

How can learning to express criticism more politely change the effect you have on the listener when speaking English? List some situations in which you think using hedging techniques can be a good idea.

Based on what you have learned about softening criticism and based on your answer to the question about Andy Warhol's kind of criticism, what kind of effect do you think his art had on the viewing public?

Link to Today

### Credit Card Companies on College Campuses—How Much Is Too Much?

One thing that students entering U.S. colleges and universities will notice is a number of companies marketing their products and services on campus. Young people have been viewed as having tremendous purchasing power since World War II, and many companies target their marketing to young people of college age. It is not uncommon to be offered a gift such as a free product or T-shirt for filling out credit card applications. This information is often sold to other marketing companies who then advertise their products and services in the mail or over the phone. It is a good idea to be careful about giving out personal information or buying things via mail, telephone, or the Internet, especially if you do not understand completely what is being offered or if your English is not very advanced. Many people, including native speakers, have been victims of marketing scams.

## Fast Facts

- In 1997, an 18-year-old University of Central Oklahoma freshman committed suicide after obtaining three credit cards without parental consent and building up a debt of $2,500.

- Owning and using a credit card within spending limits is a good way for students to build a credit history.

- The U.S. Department of Commerce reported that personal spending increased from $5.95 trillion to $6.38 trillion in 1999.

- In 1998, 67% of college students had credit cards. By 2000, the figure rose to 78%.

- It was estimated in 2001 that the average undergraduate carries a credit card balance of $2,748, while the average graduate student has $4,776 in credit card debt.

**Positive Aspects of Credit Cards**
Find and read a newspaper, magazine, or Internet article on a positive aspect of credit cards. Summarize it in your own words.

**Negative Aspects of Credit Cards**
Find and read a newspaper, magazine, or Internet article on a negative aspect of credit cards. Summarize it in your own words.

**My Personal Conclusion(s) about Credit Cards in the United States**

## Putting It All Together

This unit contained a lot of new information for you. Take some time to yourself to reflect on that information and write about the following questions. Then discuss your ideas as a class or in a small group.

1. What surprised me the most about the information regarding post-war consumer culture in the United States?

2. What does this information help me to understand about modern U.S. American life?

3. How does knowing this information change my mind about U.S. American values and attitudes?

4. Can people in other countries learn something from the effects of U.S. American consumer culture?

5. What will I tell people if I am asked about consumerism in the U.S.?

6. What kinds of positive changes can other countries make regarding consumerism? Should they make any changes at all?

# 4 The U.S. at Midcentury

## Desegregation and the Demand for Equality and Civil Rights

Dr. Martin Luther King, Jr., speaks out for civil rights. (Photo by Dick DeMarsico. Courtesy Library of Congress.)

## Net Surfers

See what information you can find by searching for the following names, words, and phrases on the World Wide Web.

Affirmative action

Affirmative action and college admissions

The American Civil War home page

The Emancipation Proclamation

Jim Crow America

Jim Crow laws

Ku Klux Klan (an Encarta encyclopedia article)

Martin Luther King, Jr.

Martin Luther King, Jr., multimedia

The Montgomery bus boycott page

1957 desegregation at Little Rock, Arkansas

Rosa Parks

Stormfront.org

## *Presidential Suite*

Dwight D. Eisenhower (R) 1953–61

John F. Kennedy (D) 1961–63

(Refer also to Abraham Lincoln (R) 1861–65)

## *On TV*

*I'll Fly Away*

## *Music Box*

"We Shall Overcome"

## *At the Movies*

*The Long Walk Home*

*Malcolm X*

*Mississippi Burning*

*To Kill a Mockingbird* (adapted from a novel)

## Preparing to Read about Desegregation and the Demand for Equality and Civil Rights

Unit 3 ended on a high note, but it is quite predictable from a historical standpoint that things might take a downswing again. Of course, this doesn't mean that things are necessarily going wrong. Many problems are solved and situations made better when people realize that there are negative things happening in society. This unit is about seeing problems and making changes for the better. Find someone in class who you don't know well yet and ask for the following information:

about racism

the racial makeup of the population in his/her community
the laws related to race in his/her community
the effect of racism on the population in his/her community

about change

the kinds of changes your classmate has seen in his/her community
the kinds of changes he/she wants to see
the changes in his/her personal life

about human rights

the human rights your classmate thinks are important
the human rights that are being denied to people in the world
the human rights your classmate is willing to fight for

Jot down the information you have learned. Discuss the information in groups of four. Be sure to check with your interview partner first to make sure there isn't any confidential information which he/she does not want to have shared with the larger group.

## Learning New Vocabulary about the U.S. at Midcentury

**discrimination (n)** exclusion based on race, gender, religion, etc.

**division (n)** split between two different things

**inequality (n)** state of not being equal or the same

**separation (n)** state of being apart from someone/something

**threat (n)** action done to scare someone

**to boycott (v)** to not use or buy a product or service; not support

**to desegregate (v)** to allow or require different people to live and work together in society

**to eliminate (v)** to get rid of

**to enforce (v)** to make sure a rule or law is followed

**to exercise (v)** to put into action

**to harvest (v)** to pick fruits, vegetables, or grains; to bring in a crop

**to integrate (v)** to put together

**to prevent (v)** to keep somebody from doing something

**to refuse (v)** to say, "I won't do it!"

**to segregate (v)** to separate

**to stand up for (v)** to support; to demand

**to upset (v)** to make someone emotionally uncomfortable or to overturn something

**to violate (v)** to break the law

**complicated (adj)** not easy; difficult to figure out

**constitutional (adj)** allowed by the U.S. Constitution; fits the ideas of the Constitution

**federal (adj)** controlled on a country-wide basis instead of by individual communities, cities, or states

**former (adj)** in the past

**local (adj)** having to do with a town or a state; immediate area

**unconstitutional (adj)** not allowed by the U.S. Constitution; against the ideas of the Constitution

## Talking about New Words and Ideas

Use your understanding of the vocabulary words to discuss the following questions with a partner or in a group.

1.  In the United States, **boycotting** has been effective in making social change. It usually works because it is based on economic factors. One national boycott was led by César Chávez. He wanted to achieve better working conditions for the grape pickers, who were mostly Hispanic. Local boycotts of businesses or products are often helpful in changing unfair practices as well, since a business needs local support to survive.

    A.  Are boycotts viewed as effective tools for change in your community?
    B.  Can you think of examples when people used boycotts to change things?
    C.  What was the reason for the boycott?
    D.  Were the goals of the boycott achieved?
    E.  Would you participate in a boycott? Why or why not?
    F.  List some words that are related to **boycott** in your mind.

2.  **Discrimination** is illegal in the United States, and you will see many public statements at businesses and schools against it. These statements often read something like: "We do not discriminate on the basis of race, nationality, ethnicity, age, gender, religion, disabilities, marital status, veteran status, sexual orientation, etc."

    A.  Are any of these kinds of discrimination accepted in your community?
    B.  Are any of these kinds of discrimination practiced in your community, regardless of laws?
    C.  Do you think that any of these kinds of discrimination are still practiced in the U.S.?
    D.  Have you experienced discrimination personally?
    E.  Do you think that more change is needed in eliminating discrimination?

    F.  What can people do to help stop discrimination?

    G.  List some words that are related to **discrimination** in your mind.

3.  If you support something or demand it, you **stand up for** it. You may notice that parents in the U.S. often encourage their children to stand up for themselves and their rights. This is considered to be a necessary skill and part of becoming an involved adult in U.S. society. It is generally not considered rude or problematic as long as the person does not break laws or harm others.

    A.  Are people encouraged or discouraged to stand up for themselves in your community?

    B.  What is the social result of demanding individual rights?

    C.  Do you think that standing up for individual rights has a positive or negative effect on society in general?

    D.  What rights of your own have you stood up for? What was the result?

    E.  List some words that are related to **standing up for something** in your mind.

4.  When things are kept apart because of laws or societal expectations, they are **segregated.** In the United States, segregation based on race is no longer legal. However, there is still some gender segregation enforced by law (such as public restrooms). Other kinds of segregation exist because of social and/or economic factors, even though there are no specific laws about it. For example, people who live in suburbs are socially segregated from people who live in inner cities, even though laws don't prevent them from interacting.

    A.  What kinds of segregation (legal or social) exist in your community?

    B.  Do people ever complain about this segregation?

    C.  What have they tried to do about it? Were they successful?

    D.  Do you see evidence of racial segregation in the United States, even though it is illegal?

    E.  List some words that are related to **segregation** in your mind.

5. When people in the same situation don't receive the same benefits or treatment there is **inequality.** Despite laws that try to eliminate inequality in the United States, many people still believe that inequality exists for social or cultural reasons. For example, many girls and young women and minorities in U.S. schools do not take advanced math and science classes even though they are allowed and encouraged to. Today, school counselors and teachers try to deal with the cultural and social reasons for this inequality by breaking stereotypes about who should take these courses.

A. Are there examples of social or cultural inequality in your community?

B. Are people satisfied with this kind of inequality? If not, what have they tried to do about it?

C. Do you think that some kinds of inequality (like gender) are determined more by society or nature?

D. Is it possible for people to eliminate inequality?

E. List some words that are related to **inequality** in your mind.

## Making Predictions about the Reading

This prediction activity has four steps. First, in a group of three, review the main ideas you discussed and the new ideas you learned about from the new vocabulary words. Together, agree on a list of five ideas that you expect to be introduced in the reading based on the information you have already. After you have done this, get together with another group. Compare your list with the other group's list. Are there some differences? Between your two groups, agree together on a final list of five ideas.

1.
2.
3.
4.
5.

Now look at the reading on civil rights to see if your group predictions were correct.

## Reading about the U.S. at Midcentury

In the mid-1800s, the United States experienced a growing **division** between the industrial states in the North and the agricultural states of the South. Whereas the northern economy was based on manufacturing, money in the South came from crops such as cotton and tobacco. Since large numbers of workers were needed to care for and **harvest** these crops, many Southerners owned slaves. This **upset** many Northerners, who felt that this practice was morally wrong. The conflict between these two ideas caused several southern states to leave the United States and form their own country—the Confederate States of America—so they could make their own laws about slavery. This, among other economic and practical issues, resulted in the U.S. Civil War, which lasted from 1861 to 1865. The North won the war, and the United States of America was one nation again, with one constitution and one common law. Earlier in 1863, President Abraham Lincoln had **eliminated** slavery in the Union States with the Emancipation Proclamation, a **federal** document stating that the **former** slaves were U.S.

A clear Civil War division line between North and South near Chattanooga, Tennessee, 1864. (Courtesy DoD Visual Information Record Center.)

President Abraham Lincoln signed the Emancipation Proclamation. (Photo by Matthew Brady. Courtesy DoD Visual Information Record Center.)

citizens who were free to live and work where and how they chose. This was reinforced by the Thirteenth Amendment. The Confederate states didn't honor this until the war was over.

When the slaves were freed, many moved to the North. But even as late as 1950, two-thirds of the African American population still lived in the South. Even though slavery no longer existed, many black citizens still faced social and political **discrimination.** Since the passage of the Thirteenth Amendment, every U.S. citizen is expected to accept the citizenship of African Americans. However, each state also has the right to make its own laws if there are no federal laws on an issue. This is how the Ku Klux Klan and "Jim Crow laws" became stronger in some Southern states. These laws were made by local leaders in individual states to keep blacks and whites away from each other in public areas without **violating** federal laws. Jim Crow laws legally forced blacks and whites to use separate public restrooms, separate drinking fountains, and separate waiting rooms. Trains, buses, and restaurants had "whites only" and "colored only" sections. Black children were not allowed to go to school with white children. **Complicated** rules stating that people could vote only if their grandparents had voted and **threats** to blacks by whites **prevented** many African American citizens from **exercising** their legal voting rights.

The separation caused by Jim Crow laws was questioned in many courts. The U.S. Supreme Court had ruled as early as 1892 that "separate but equal" was **constitutional.** This meant that it was legal in the U.S. for different facilities to exist for blacks and whites, as long as they were of similar quality. African American leaders such as Dr. Martin Luther King, Jr., claimed that such separation created **inequality.** King encouraged his followers **to stand up for** equal rights through peaceful protest. In 1954, the Supreme Court ruled that "separate but equal" was **unconstitutional.**

The next logical step was to **integrate** the schools. In the 1954 case of *Brown* v. *Board of Education* in Topeka, Kansas, the Supreme Court ruled that school **segregation** was unconstitutional. The first attempt to integrate schools was at Little Rock, Arkansas, where the governor brought in the Arkansas National Guard soldiers to block the door and prevent nine black children from attending a school for white children. President Eisenhower sent soldiers from the federal army to take the students to class. Despite this, efforts to integrate schools were slow. The most public and symbolic beginning of the civil rights movement took place in Montgomery, Alabama. In 1955, Rosa Parks (an African American U.S. citizen) boarded a bus and sat in the "whites only" section. When asked to move, she **refused** and was arrested by the police. Because of her arrest and the discrimination of the bus company, blacks organized a year-long **boycott** of the buses, causing the bus company to lose a lot of money. But even this was not enough to convince the bus company. Eventually, the Supreme Court declared segregation of transportation unconstitutional.

Despite these small victories, some universities in the Deep South remained all-white as late as 1963. Governor George C. Wallace of Alabama stood in the doorway of the University of Alabama shouting, "Segregation now! Segregation tomorrow! Segregation forever!" to prevent two African American students from taking classes at the university. Again, federal troops had to **enforce** the law. Although many people today believe that U.S. schools and American society are desegregated, others argue that inequality still exists. While no society will ever be perfect, the vision and courage of many civil rights leaders and supporters brought the United States much closer to its original ideal of equality.

## Responding to Information about Desegregation and the Demand for Equality and Civil Rights

What did you think about the information in this reading? Many students are surprised to know that things were so divided in U.S. American society. Were you? How can you use this information in your life? One way to help us use information from reading is to make connections from the reading to ourselves. What does the information in the text remind you of in your personal life? Write a paragraph about it.

## Understanding the Reading: Comprehension Check

In this unit, you're going to take a multiple choice test. The multiple choice test is even more popular than the true/false test because it is just as quick and easy to score for large numbers of people, but it does a better job of separating the students who know the material from those who don't. With four or five answer choices instead of only two, I'm sure you can see why. If you have already taken the TOEFL exam, you have already experienced this testing technique. If you will be studying in the United States, it will be helpful to understand how this test works. A multiple choice test is set up so that each question contains a "stem" and four or five answer choices. The correct choice is the answer, and the others are called "distractors." Usually, one distractor is obviously wrong while the other two are more or less possible. The goal of the multiple choice test is to choose the best answer. Use your understanding of the reading to eliminate the distractors and to circle the one best answer for each question.

1. A Jim Crow law is

    a. a law against shooting birds.
    b. a law forcing racial separation in public.
    c. a law making slavery illegal.
    d. a law separating children at school.

2. African American children living in the Southern U.S. in the early 1950s were *not* allowed to

   a. go to school.
   b. go to school with other black children.
   c. go to school with white children.
   d. go to school on a bus.

3. The phrase "separate but equal" means

   a. different public places for black and white citizens were constitutional if the quality was similar.
   b. different public places for black and white citizens were not constitutional.
   c. different public places for black and white citizens were not equal.
   d. different public places for black and white citizens did not exist.

4. The bus company in Montgomery, Alabama, began allowing African Americans to sit wherever they wanted to on their buses because

   a. they were forced to by a Supreme Court decision.
   b. they lost so much money when African Americans stopped riding the bus.
   c. they were concerned about the comfort of all customers.
   d. they got a lot of bad publicity from Rosa Parks's arrest.

5. Desegregation laws in U.S. American schools resulted in

   a. protests by whites.
   b. protests by blacks.
   c. protests by the government.
   d. protests by the teachers.

6. The first school in the United States to be desegregated was located in

   a. Montgomery, Alabama.
   b. Topeka, Kansas.
   c. Little Rock, Arkansas.
   d. Hooper, Utah.

7. The governor of Arkansas tried to prevent nine black children from attending school by

    a. holding the front door open to them.
    b. telling them to go home.
    c. standing in the doorway shouting, "Segregation forever!"
    d. bringing in Arkansas National Guard soldiers to block the doorway.

8. In order to make sure that black children were allowed into white schools, President Eisenhower

    a. sent federal troops to accompany the students to class.
    b. had a friendly chat with the Arkansas governor.
    c. signed a new federal bill requiring schools to register black children.
    d. did nothing and hoped for the best.

9. When did the University of Alabama begin to allow black students to study there?

    a. 1863
    b. 1950
    c. 1955
    d. 1963

10. The phrase that best describes racial attitudes in the United States after World War II is

    a. open and tolerant
    b. bitter and helpless
    c. confused but progressive
    d. joyful but painful

How did you do on the multiple choice? It's OK if you didn't get them all right. In addition to learning cultural and historical information, you are also learning about U.S. American testing styles, which is also an important aspect of culture. The important thing now is whether you understood the reading. If you really don't think you got the reading, please go back and look at it again before we move on. Apply your new mastery of the reading to a famous speech given at the Lincoln Memorial in Washington, D.C., on August 28, 1963, by Dr. Martin Luther King, Jr.

## "I Have a Dream!": Reading a Speech by Dr. Martin Luther King, Jr.

Have you ever had a dream for your world? Your country? Yourself? Dr. Martin Luther King, Jr., had a dream for the United States of America. His famous "I Have a Dream" speech is available on the web from a variety of historical or civil rights sites. The paragraph starting with the words "I have a dream that one day this nation will rise up . . ." is the most famous part of this speech. Read it and answer the questions that follow.

What is King's main message to the people?

Do you think that his dream came true in the United States? Give one example of how his dream came true. Give one example of how it has not.

Listen to the entire speech if you can. What do you notice about the way King delivers the speech? What kind of body language and voice does he use? What effect does it have on the listener?

**Language Focus**

## Using Parallelism to Talk about Our Own Dreams

Did you like the speech? It is a very strong speech, and many U.S. Americans associate the word ***dream*** with the ideas of this speech. One linguistic/rhetorical factor that makes King's speech very focused on the dream is that he repeated the same introductory phrase "I have a dream that . . ." several times. This is a technique called ***parallelism,*** and it is used by speakers and writers of English to focus the listener's or reader's attention. Did it work for you? Was King able to keep your attention focused on his dream?

Many people have dreams. Some may want to be famous or rich. Others may be more concerned with world issues and dream of a world with no war or hunger. Dreams are an important part of life. What is your dream? Write a speech about your own dreams, using parallelism when possible to keep the listener/reader focused on your dream.

I have a dream that one day . . .

I have a dream that people will be able to . . .

I have a dream today . . .

Deliver your speech to your classmates.

## Understanding More about Thoughts on Civil Rights: Conducting a Survey

What is your opinion on civil rights? What do your international classmates think? What do American students in your community think? How can you find out? Surveys are a good way to get information about people's attitudes toward various ideas. You will notice that surveys play an important part of life in the United States. Newspapers often report results of polling information, consumer groups often survey customers at local shopping centers, and organizations sometimes call and conduct telephone surveys on various topics. Many Americans are happy to answer survey questions if they have time and if the surveyor is polite and gives a little personal information about why they are conducting a survey. Most, however, do not like to be surveyed over the phone. U.S. students tend to be very willing to help out if they know that the information is used for a class project. Keep in mind, though, that race issues can be very sensitive in any population.

Make copies of the following survey and ask your classmates as well as trusted English native speakers such as roommates, fellow students in classes, etc. Compare the answers of those who have not lived in the U.S. for very long and those who have.

**Civil Rights Survey**

1. The civil rights movement was one of the most important periods in American history.

   Strongly Agree      Agree      Neutral      Disagree      Strongly Disagree

2. The United States has solved its problems with racial discrimination.

   Strongly Agree      Agree      Neutral      Disagree      Strongly Disagree

3. The government needs to do more to eliminate social and economic segregation.

   Strongly Agree      Agree      Neutral      Disagree      Strongly Disagree

4. Each individual is responsible for any segregation/discrimination that still exists.

   Strongly Agree      Agree      Neutral      Disagree      Strongly Disagree

5. The United States must keep all laws that protect minority citizens.

   Strongly Agree      Agree      Neutral      Disagree      Strongly Disagree

Is there anything that surprises you about the survey results?

**Link to Today**

## Affirmative Action and College Admissions—Who Should Go to College?

Affirmative action laws were one result of the civil rights movement. They were designed to help minorities and women to get an education and get jobs by guaranteeing that those who are qualified are given preference in college admissions and job hiring. These laws were supposed to help create racial and gender balance in America's top schools and jobs by giving extra admissions points to minorities and to females in male-dominated programs. However, many people argued that it was "reverse discrimination," which made it difficult for qualified white males to get positions.

Affirmative action has become very controversial. In 1996, California citizens voted "yes" on Proposition 209. This state law was designed to eliminate affirmative action, making it illegal to give racial preference in California university admissions; now, admissions are based only on grades and test scores. Opponents have argued that the tests are racially biased and that all of the progress made by women and minorities since the civil rights movement will disappear. Other states are considering similar laws, and many challenges are being made in state and federal courts. The U.S. Supreme Court will need to determine a national policy.

## Fast Facts

- A University of Michigan applicant who was denied admission filed a lawsuit in 1997, accusing the university of turning her down to make room for "less-qualified" minority students. Legal action is pending.

- Without affirmative action policies, the admissions numbers for African American and Hispanic students at the University of California, Berkeley, dropped sharply in 1998.

- Due to budget cuts in 1997, a high school in Piscataway, N.J., that was forced to let one of its teachers go, chose to keep the African American teacher for the sake of diversity. The white teacher filed a reverse discrimination lawsuit in court and lost.

- In 1999, the University of Washington reported a decline in the number of applications from African American, American Indian, and Hispanic students while Asian American student admission rates were up slightly.

- The University of Georgia announced an increase in minority enrollments for 2001, up from the previous year.

**Positive Aspects of Affirmative Action**
Find and read a newspaper, magazine, or Internet article on a positive aspect of affirmative action. Summarize it in your own words.

**Negative Aspects of Affirmative Action**
Find and read a newspaper, magazine, or Internet article on a negative aspect of affirmative action. Summarize it in your own words.

**My Personal Conclusion(s) about Affirmative Action in the United States**

## Putting It All Together

Think about what you have learned in this unit and how it relates to your personal life, your culture, or the world around you. First, take some time to write down your ideas about these questions. Then, in groups of three, talk about the following questions and/or others you may have. When you have discussed your ideas as a group, you should present them to the whole class.

1. What surprised me the most about the civil rights movement?

2. What does this information help me to understand about modern U.S. American life?

3. How does knowing about desegregation and civil rights change my mind about U.S. American values and attitudes?

4. Can people in other countries learn something from the lessons U.S. Americans took from the civil rights movement?

5. What will I tell people in my country now if they ask me about race issues in the United States?

6. What kinds of positive changes can other countries make regarding racial discrimination? Should my country make changes at all?

# 5 The U.S. Counterrevolution of the Sixties

## Sex, Drugs, and Rock 'n' Roll

Poster for Woodstock Festival. (Courtesy Library of Congress.)

## Net Surfers

See what information you can find by searching for the following names, words, and phrases on the World Wide Web.

Beat writers

Family life education

Hippies

Jack Kerouac

Jack Kerouac's world

Martin's Route 66 gallery and essay

National Historic Route 66 Federation

1960s guides and directories

Postcards from Route 66

Sex education

Sixties word list

Teen pregnancy prevention

## *Presidential Suite*

John F. Kennedy (D) 1961–63
Lyndon B. Johnson (D) 1963–69
Richard M. Nixon (R) 1969–74

## *On TV*

*The Wonder Years*

## *Music Box*

"Aquarius" - The Fifth Dimension
"Blowin' in the Wind" - Bob Dylan
"Route 66" - Bobby Troupe
"San Francisco" - Scott McKenzie
"The Times They Are A-Changin'" - Bob Dylan
"Turn, Turn, Turn" - The Byrds
"Volunteers" - Jefferson Airplane

## Preparing to Read about Sex, Drugs, and Rock 'n' Roll

The sixties is known as the era of the counterrevolution and is one of the most popular and romanticized eras of twentieth century U.S. American life. Based on your knowledge of prior units, you may be surprised to hear that U.S. Americans were still struggling to solve problems and make changes in the sixties, just as they were in the time period of the last unit. This is probably because the ideas and problems in this unit are results of the consumer culture. Instead of interviewing classmates, take some time to write down your ideas

about hippies
the way they look
the way they dress
the way they think

about authority
the authorities in your own life
the reaction you have to authority
the results of not obeying authority

about sex
the public attitudes about sex in your community
the conflict between conservative and liberal attitudes about sex
the attitudes you have personally about sex

Since it is always so interesting to find out about what everybody else is thinking, you should share some of your ideas with your classmates before we move on to learning the new vocabulary words. As always, it's okay if you want to keep some of your private thoughts to yourself.

## Learning New Vocabulary about the U.S. Counterrevolution of the Sixties

**activism (n)** belief in making social changes according to one's ideas

**basis (n)** the core or foundation of something; idea something is built on

**beatnik (n)** member of the "beat" generation of the 1950s–'60s. The "beat" generation was critical of society and expressed their ideas

**commune (n)** shared living situation involving unrelated people; everyone gives what they have and takes what they need

**consumerism (n)** attitude that values consuming instead of saving or preserving

**counterrevolution (n)** movement to make U.S. American society more liberal and open; also called the Hippie Movement

**disillusionment (n)** loss of belief in one's faith, country, government, parents, society, etc.

**establishment (n)** something that is a foundation of society; schools and institutions are good examples

**flower child (n)** name given to the less political, more romantic hippies

**hippie (n)** Representative of the counterrevolution—a liberal member of society, especially that in the 1960s

**materialism (n)** attitude that values money and purchased items

**opportunity (n)** the chance to do something

**public (n)** outside of the home or private life (more often used as an adjective)

**restlessness (n)** need to go to different places and try different things; inability to settle down into a routine

**romanticism (n)** dreamy and idealistic attitude

**sex, drugs & rock 'n' roll (n)** phrase that represents what was thought to be the themes of the era of the counterrevolution

**sexism (n)** belief that men are better than women (or vice versa)

**teach-in (n)** a gathering of protesters who sit in large groups and educate the public about their ideas and goals

**to drop out (v)** to stop attending school; to stop participating in society (*dropout* is the noun)

**to further (v)** to help something grow bigger, stronger, or more visible

**to hitchhike (v)** to travel by asking for a ride from other people, most often strangers

**to realize (v)** to come to understand or see something that you did not before

### Talking about New Words and Ideas

Use your understanding of the vocabulary words to discuss the following questions with a partner or in a group.

1. Since World War II, the United States has been the leader in **consumerism,** using the most raw materials and natural resources in the world. Most of the new jobs created in the U.S. are in the service industry. A growing number of people are beginning to worry about the social and environmental effects of this trend.

   A. What effects of consumerism do you see in U.S. society?
   B. Do you think that these effects will create problems in the future?
   C. How do people in your community view American consumerism?
   D. Do you think that your country is becoming more consumer-oriented?
   E. If this is a problem in your community, what can you and those around you do to stop it or at least slow it down?
   F. List any words that are related to **consumerism** in your mind.

2. **Sexism** refers to the belief that men are better than women or that women are better than men and practices that come from or support that idea. Sexist attitudes especially bother the majority of American women, who expect to be treated with respect and equality both in public and at home.

   A. Can you think of examples of sexism in the United States?
   B. Does sexism exist in your community? What evidence do you see that it does or does not?

C.  How can people make changes that allow more equality between men and women? Should they make such changes? Why or why not?

D.  List any words that are related to **sexism** in your mind.

3.  The word **establishment** refers to the individual institutions that make a community, such as businesses, schools, and churches. In the 1960s, the hippies used this word to describe the traditional codes of white, male-dominated America. Most of the rebellion of this time period was directed against "the establishment." The adjective *established* is used today to refer to ideas that are common to the culture of the U.S. and generally understood by its citizens.

A.  What are some ideas that seem to be established in U.S. society?

B.  Are the established ideas in your community similar to these ideas or different?

C.  Do you believe that the established ideas of your community are too rigid or too flexible? If so, is it possible for people to make a change? How?

D.  List any words that are related to the **establishment** in your mind.

4.  In the 1960s, a common form of protest was called a **teach-in.** This was a peaceful activity, mostly on university campuses, where students sat together and talked about their viewpoints on various issues instead of going to class. Often, student activists (politically involved leaders of the hippie movement) would teach the others about the issues concerning them and ask other students for support in protesting them.

A.  Do you think that this kind of activism is effective?

B.  Are young people or students in your community allowed to organize or to participate in such activities? Why or why not? What usually happens if people protest?

C.  Can you imagine yourself at an activity similar to a teach-in?

D.  List any words that are related to a **teach-in** in your mind.

5.  When people lose faith in any aspect of their government, family, or selves, they are experiencing **disillusionment.** The hippies had little faith in the ability of the older generations or of the government

to make the right legal, moral, and social decisions for them to follow. They rejected the old values and searched for better ways of doing things. This is common in every generation, but it was never as public nor as organized as it was in 1960s America as the large baby boom generation became adults.

A. Do you think that Americans are disillusioned today? What evidence do you see of this?
B. Are you disillusioned with any aspect of your life?
C. Are the young people in your community disillusioned with your government? If so, what evidence do you see of this?
D. Can people reject the old ways and make a change? Should they?
E. List any words that are related to **disillusionment** in your mind.

6. Even today, a person who is idealistic and does not conform to the materialistic consumerism in U.S. society is often teasingly called a **flower child.** Some young people today imitate this style and use it as part of their own identity.

A. Do you know anybody who acts like a flower child?
B. Is there another name in your community for such a person? Are you such a person?
C. How are such people treated in your community?
D. Can this kind of person help your community? How?
E. List any words that are related to a **flower child** in your mind.

## Making Predictions about the Reading

In a small group of three, review the main ideas you discussed along with the photos at the beginning of the unit and the new ideas you learned about from the vocabulary words. Without looking at the reading, make a list of seven ideas that you expect to be introduced in the reading based on the information you have already. Then get together with a second group of three and agree on the seven ideas you think will be in the reading. Don't write your ideas down until everybody in both groups agrees.

1.
2.
3.
4.
5.
6.
7.

Did you agree with the other group or was there heated discussion? In any case, what is important is that you thought about the reading ahead of time and talked about it. Let's see how you did on your list of seven ideas.

## Reading about the U.S. Counterrevolution of the Sixties

After World War II, the economy in the United States was better than it had ever been. People began to have extra money that they spent on houses, large appliances such as washing machines and dryers, and cars. This wealth in the 1950s created a consumer culture in which **materialism** and **consumerism** were valued. However, many felt that this system favored white, male Americans and kept minorities and women in lower social positions. Protest against attitudes of racism and sexism by the **establishment** culture was the **basis** of the hippie movement, also known as the counterrevolution. When young people **realized** that American society was still based on **sexism** and racism, they rebelled. The U.S. government's decision to send more and more troops to fight in the Vietnam War increased the student protests.

A new, negative feeling about authority began to spread among the youth. "Don't trust anyone over thirty!" became a popular attitude among the younger generation as they protested consumer materialism and the war in Vietnam. In addition to the social **activism** of focused political protests and **teach-ins,** other young **flower children** were less focused, experimenting with drugs and teaching peace and harmony instead of conflict and war. The literature of this generation depicted the **restlessness** and **disillusionment** of the hippies, some of whom drifted from coast to coast in search of a new way of life. However, despite the **romanticism** linked to this time period, many dedicated people risked their futures and even their lives for social change.

During this time, traditional family structures and religious moral values broke down rapidly, changing the structure of American society. Many students **dropped out** of school, and some young people left home to live in **communes.** Men grew their hair long. Men and women began to feel less of a need for marriage (it was part of the establishment) and became more open about sexuality. The introduction of the birth control pill **furthered** this movement. The feminist movement began during this time and grew stronger in the 1970s. Women wanted challenging jobs outside of the home and protested for equality at work. The National Organization for Women was founded in 1966, and gender discrimination by employers was made illegal under President Johnson, opening up more job **opportunities** and equal pay for women.

## Responding to Information about Sex, Drugs, and Rock 'n' Roll

How did you do with your predictions this time? Another important reading skill is the ability to relate this reading to what you have read or seen in another text. A text can be anything from a book or poem to a cartoon, TV commercial, or words to a song. In the last unit, we wrote about how the information in the reading reminded us of connections to ourselves. In this unit you are going to make connections between this reading and another text in English or your native language. Was there a part in the reading that reminded you of a book, poem, movie, etc.? Use the space provided below to jot down your ideas about it. Then, give a three- to five-minute presentation to the class, showing the relationship between the two texts. Be sure to give specific details.

## Understanding the Reading: Comprehension Check

This comprehension check is similar to that in Unit 2. This time though, instead of choosing the best word, you get to think of the best word yourself. Although this is a little more difficult than before, there is no exact right or wrong answer. Fill in the blanks with any word that shows your understanding of the reading. (The abbreviations in parentheses indicate the part of speech needed: *n = noun; v = verb; adj = adjective.*)

The good postwar economy, in addition to creating a wealthy consumer society, also created a system that valued (n) _____ . Young people thought that this system was (adj) _____ and they were (adj) _____ toward the establishment and authority. Young people experimented with (n) _____ . Some (v) _____ around the country. Many view the time of the hippies as (adj) _____ , but this was not always realistic. Social activism and protesting caused (n) _____ for some young people. Traditions such as marriage and family structure began to (v) _____ and young people (v) _____ . The feminist movement began at this time because women wanted (n) _____ .

Check your answers with your classmates and your instructor. Although many of you used different words, I am sure that most of you still were able to show your understanding of the reading. People understand things differently because of their personal experiences and choose different words to express that. Let's look at the experiences of two literary characters in the 1960s and the words that the author, Jack Kerouac, used to describe them.

## *On the Road:* Looking at a Novel by Jack Kerouac

We learned earlier that the literature of the hippie generation talked about restlessness and disillusionment. A famous American novel written by Jack Kerouac reflects the "beat" generation and their restlessness in the 1950s and '60s. In the novel, the two main characters hitchhike back and forth across the United States, meeting many new people and experiencing the various aspects of the counterculture. They are disillusioned with the establishment and are searching for a new way to live their lives. They get many new ideas from the people they meet. The following paragraph from the novel *On the Road* tells us what kind of people the characters in the book meet, the places they see, and the adventures they have. In this part of the novel, they have just finished traveling across the country from the East Coast. They have arrived in Los Angeles, where everybody is hanging around and doing their own thing. They have very little money left from their long journey.

South Main Street, where Terry and I took strolls [*go for a walk*] with hot dogs, was a fantastic carnival of lights and wildness. Booted cops [*police*] frisked [*check for drugs or weapons*] people on practically every corner. The beatest characters [*those most representing hippie (beatnik) attitudes*] in all the country swarmed [*moving around in mass*] the sidewalks—all of it under those Southern California stars that are lost in the brown halo of the huge desert encampment L.A. really is. You could smell the tea, weed, I mean, marijuana [*illegal drug in the United States*] floating in the air, together with chili beans and beer. That grand wild sound of bop [*a kind of jazz music*] floated from the beer parlors, it mixed medleys [*combination of sounds*] with every kind of cowboy and boogie-woogie in the American night. Everybody looked like Hassel. Wild Negroes with bop caps and goatees [*small, pointed chin beard*] came laughing by; the long haired brokendown hipsters [*jazz fans*] straight off Route 66 from New York; then old desert rats, carrying packs and heading for a park bench at the plaza; then Methodist ministers with raveled sleeves, and an occasional Nature Boy saint in beard and sandals. I wanted to meet them all, talk to everybody, but Terry and I were too busy trying to get a buck [*some money*] together. (72–73)

1. Make a list of adjectives to describe the mood in this paragraph.

2. What details in the paragraph are similar to the reading on the counterrevolution earlier in the chapter?

3. What kind of people are described in the paragraph? Do you think they are like typical U.S. Americans today? Why or why not?

### Telling about Our Own Experiences on the Road

In the last sentence of the paragraph, the characters are "trying to get a buck together." This is a way of saying that they were out of money and needed to find a way to get some. Have you ever traveled somewhere and needed some money? Maybe you went across town and forgot your wallet or purse. Or maybe you were on a long trip far away and ran out of cash. What did you do? How did you get the money you needed? Tell the story to a classmate or your whole class in the past tense. Describe the people and the surroundings. Explain how you finally got the money you needed.

## Using Less Direct Speech in Making Our Own Requests

In Unit 3, we learned about expressing critique indirectly by using hedging techniques. Making requests is another speech act that benefits from less directness. Many U.S. American speakers of English think it is rude to make direct requests or demands and prefer to work with people who are less direct in their approach. Here are some direct and indirect requests for money. Number them in order from the *most* direct to the *least* direct.

   \_\_\_ "Could you lend me some money?"

   \_\_\_ "I need some money."

   \_\_\_ "Give me money!"

   \_\_\_ "May I have some of your money?"

   \_\_\_ "You'd better give me some money!"

   \_\_\_ "Would it be possible for you to lend me some money?"

   \_\_\_ "Put the money in the bag!"

What can you say if you need a book? Some help with directions? To borrow your friend's bike? Order your answers from *most* direct to *least* direct.

| Need a Book from a Librarian | Need Help with Directions from a Stranger | Need to Borrow a Bike from a Friend |
|---|---|---|
| 1. | 1. | 1. |
| 2. | 2. | 2. |
| 3. | 3. | 3. |
| 4. | 4. | 4. |
| 5. | 5. | 5. |

Of the stranger, the librarian, and the friend, who can you be most direct with?

Who should you be least direct with?

## Applying What We've Learned from *On the Road:* Traveling Route 66

In Jack Kerouac's novel *On the Road,* the two main characters arrived in L.A. via Route 66. This is the name of the most famous road in America, nicknamed "the Main Street of America" and "the Mother Road." Connecting Chicago with Los Angeles, it is 2448 miles (4000 km) long and crosses eight states and three time zones. Prior to interstate freeway travel, this two-lane highway was a primary means of crossing the United States by car. Look at the map of Route 66 and trace its path from east to west. Route 66 crosses through 10 major U.S. cities. From east to west, list the cities and their states here.

1.                          6.

2.                          7.

3.                          8.

4.                          9.

5.                          10.

A sign from Route 66 as it passes through New Mexico

Using an encyclopedia from a library or the Internet, look up information about each of these cities and the states in which they are located.

- What are the main attractions in each city?
- What is the population?
- What is the climate?
- What is the geography/landscape like?
- What do most people in the area do for a living?

What major changes in population and geography can you find by tracing Route 66 from east to west?

## Sex Education at School—Contraception or Abstinence?

One major part of the counterrevolution was the sexual revolution in the United States. Because the United States is a nation founded by people seeking freedom to practice religion as they chose, it is generally considered to be a Protestant nation with corresponding values. The publically accepted image of American sexual behavior up until the counterrevolution was a picture of abstinence before marriage and fidelity within marriage. (In reality, this was not always the case.) However, these values were questioned by the generation of "free love" and the freedom created by the availability of birth control which caused the public image of sexual behavior to become more liberal. In July 2001, the U.S. surgeon general issued a report calling for a program of public education about sexual health that integrates family, community, and religious values with medical knowledge and services to prevent sexually transmitted disease and unwanted pregnancy while promoting the sexual well-being of U.S. citizens.

A battle about the role that public schools should play in sex education continues to rage in the United States. Public officials, citing the highest teen pregnancy rates in the industrialized world and the threat of AIDS and other sexually transmitted diseases, insist that it is the school's job to educate teens about sexuality and contraception. Some parents claim that the schools are taking away their right to educate their children in the home. Many parents insist that teens should be taught abstinence before marriage and that teaching students about contraception encourages them to adopt different morals than parents are teaching. Because education is considered a local issue and not a federal one, many different policies about sex education exist in U.S. schools.

## Fast Facts

- The National Centers for Disease Control in Atlanta, Georgia, estimated in 1996 that 53% of high school students have had sex before graduation.

- According to the Centers for Disease Control, teen pregnancy rates dropped to a record low in 1997.

- In 1998, the Virginia House of Representatives passed legislation to restore mandatory sex education in schools.

- The U.S. Surgeon General David Satcher stressed information about both abstinence and contraception in his 2001 sex education report.

**Positive Aspects of Sex Education in School**
Find and read a newspaper, magazine, or Internet article on a positive aspect of sex education in school. Summarize it in your own words.

**Negative Aspects of Sex Education in School**
Find and read a newspaper, magazine, or Internet article on a negative aspect of sex education in school. Summarize it in your own words.

**My Personal Conclusion(s) about Sex Education in U.S. Schools**

## Putting It All Together

Take a moment to yourself and write down your ideas about these questions. Then, in groups of three, talk about the following questions and/or others you might have.

1. What surprised me most about the information on the counter-revolution?

2. What does the information help me to understand about U.S. American life?

3. How does knowing this information change my mind about U.S. American values and attitudes?

4. Can people in my community learn something from the experiences U.S. Americans had with the counterrevolution?

5. What will I tell people now if they ask me about hippies in the United States?

6. What kinds of positive changes can my community make regarding social structures? Should these changes be made at all?

# 6 The U.S. in the Cold War Era

## Defending Democracy from McCarthy to Vietnam

President Johnson greets U.S. troops in Vietnam in 1966. (Courtesy DoD Visual Information Record Center.)

## Net Surfers

See what information you can find by searching for the following names, words, and phrases on the World Wide Web.

Berlin airlift

CNN Cold War

Cold War hot links

GI Bill Express.com

Marshall Plan

The Red Scare 1945 to 1954

ROTC home

Senator Joseph McCarthy— a multimedia celebration

Veterans

Vietnam Veterans Memorial

Vietnam Women's Memorial Project

## *Presidential Suite*

Harry S Truman (D) 1945–53

Dwight D. Eisenhower (R) 1953–61

John F. Kennedy (D) 1961–63

Lyndon B. Johnson (D) 1963–69

Richard M. Nixon (R) 1969–74

Gerald R. Ford (R) 1974–77

## *On TV*

*All in the Family*

*China Beach*

*M*A*S*H*

## *Music Box*

"Fortunate Son" - Creedence Clearwater Revival

"Where Have All the Flowers Gone?" - Pete Seeger

---

## *At the Movies*

*Apocalypse Now*
*Born on the Fourth of July*
*Coming Home*
*Full Metal Jacket*
*Platoon*
*The Deer Hunter*
*Thirteen Days*

---

## Preparing to Read about Defending Democracy from McCarthy to Vietnam

In Unit 6 discussions, things in the U.S. remain much the same, with lots of protests and efforts to deal with problems at home and overseas. That is mostly because the events in this unit overlap with Unit 4, which dealt primarily with the 1950s, and with Unit 5, which dealt with the 1960s. Instead of the domestic social issues of the other two units, though, this unit focuses on political/ideological issues from the 1950s through the 1970s. During those decades, the Vietnam War was an important crisis in the U.S. foreign policy. This unit explores the domestic and foreign affairs that stemmed from the country's belief in the primacy of democracy. But first, let's see what you and your classmates have to say

about communism/socialism
the knowledge your classmate has about communism/socialism
your classmate's attitude toward communism/socialism

about democracy
the knowledge your classmate has about democracy
your classmate's attitude toward democracy

about ideology
the types of ideology promoted in his/her community
the types of ideology he/she experienced in childhood (at school, church, home, etc.)
the attitude he/she has toward public ideologies today

Based on the questions listed above, ask two follow-up questions of your interview partner.

1.

2.

## Learning New Vocabulary about the U.S. in the Cold War Era

**cold war (n)** a war of beliefs between East and West, represented by the "superpowers" of the former Soviet Socialist Republics (USSR) and the United States. The cold war ended with the fall of the Berlin Wall in 1989 and the collapse of the Soviet Union.

**communism (n)** a political belief that promotes state control of most resources and public distribution of funds in society

**concern (n)** a worry or fear

**democracy (n)** a political belief that promotes private control of most resources and private distribution of funds in society

**exploration (n)** a state of investigating or looking at new things

**population (n)** the people who live in an area, city, or country

**presence (n)** the state of being somewhere

**scorn (n)** extreme dislike or disapproval

**sympathy (n)** having positive feelings or understanding about something or someone

**veteran (n)** a person who has served the U.S. in a war

**to accuse (v)** to point a finger at; blame somebody for an action

**to assassinate (v)** to murder a famous person—often a political leader—by surprise attack

**to be associated with (v)** to have connections with or to be related to

**to declare (v)** to state or say something

**to draft (v)** to force someone to fight in a war

**to drive (v)** to be the force behind an idea or action

**to extend (v)** to go beyond the original action or state

**to flood (v)** to fill an area

**to recognize (v)** to give somebody credit for doing something

**to suspect (v)** to have an unproven idea or impression

**domestic (adj)** at home; in politics refers to within the United States

**struggling (adj)** having difficulty

**surrounding (adj)** things near or next to something else

**violent (adj)** causing extreme harm or injury

### Talking about New Words and Ideas

Use your understanding of the vocabulary words to discuss the following questions with a partner or in a group.

1. **Communism** and **democracy** are political ideologies. An ideology shapes the thinking and the activities of large groups of people, such as a religious group or a government. Human beings group themselves together based on ideologies.

    A. Explain your understanding of democracy.
    B. Explain your understanding of communism.
    C. Are ideologies helpful or harmful to human beings? Both? Explain how.
    D. List any words that are related to **democracy** and **communism** in your mind

2. **A riot** is caused when a large group of people become violent. This can either be due to premeditated protesting, as was the case in Los Angeles in 1994 when members of various ethnic groups protested the verdict in the case of police brutality against Rodney King, or it can happen somewhat accidentally when large crowds of people become excited at or about concerts or sporting events. This was the case in Tucson, Arizona, in April 2001 when University of Arizona basketball fans became upset when their team lost to Duke University in the national championships.

    A. Have there ever been riots in your community or city that you remember? What was the reason for the riot?

B. Have you ever been involved in a riot? If so, was it intentional or accidental?

C. Do you think rioting is an effective way to demonstrate for what you believe in?

D. List any words that are related to **riot** in your mind.

3. A **witch hunt** is a term used when people in power seek out those who do not believe the same way they do and cause those people bodily or emotional harm. Today, this is mostly a political event. However, in the 17th century, anyone who was not liked in the community or broke the rules in some way could be accused of being a witch by his/her neighbors. A public trial would be held that often involved the accused "proving" that he/she was not a witch by performing some act such as walking on hot coals. If the suspected person witch did not get burned, this was proof that the victim was not human and, therefore, was indeed a witch.

A. Has anything similar to a witch hunt ever happened in your community's history? If so, explain as many details as you can.

B. Could something like a witch hunt happen in your community today? In the future?

C. Have you noticed any examples of such behavior in smaller forms?

D. What do you think causes people to accuse others for their beliefs?

E. What can you do to help make sure that people are not falsely accused?

F. List any words that are related to the term **witch hunt** in your mind.

4. When a planned attack against a public official or leader occurs and that person dies, it is referred to as an **assassination.** Four U.S. presidents have been assassinated: Abraham Lincoln, James Garfield, William McKinley, and John F. Kennedy. Attempted assassinations were committed against Presidents Gerald Ford and Ronald Reagan. In addition, Martin Luther King, Jr., and Senator Robert F. Kennedy were both assassinated in 1968.

A. Can you think of other world or local leaders who were assassinated? Who? Do you know who did it and why?

B. Is it justifiable to assassinate a leader because you do not believe in him/her? Why or why not?

C. Is it justifiable to assassinate a leader who is harming the people? Why or why not?

D. List any words that are related to **assassination** in your mind.

5. When you feel that you owe it to somebody to do something for him/her you feel **bound** to help or do something for that person. We can feel obligated for many reasons, including ideology, political ties, religious ties, family ties, or personal experience to name a few.

A. Have you ever felt bound to do something for somebody? What was the situation?

B. Have you ever been bound to do something for somebody, but did not? What was the situation? Did you feel bad? Why or why not?

C. Do you think being bound to do certain things can be dangerous or harmful sometimes? Give examples.

D. List any words that are related to being **bound**.

## Making Predictions about the Reading

In a group of three, review the main ideas you discussed and the new ideas you learned about from the new vocabulary words. Without looking at the reading, think of four ideas that you expect to be introduced in the reading based on the information you have already. Then, get together with two other groups of three and agree together on your list before you write them down. This will be a little harder than in the other units because you must agree on fewer list items.

1.
2.
3.
4.

How did you do? You probably noticed that more people and fewer ideas equals more negotiation. While you are demonstrating your skill at predicting, you are also negotiating in English. This is another great activity in a foreign language learning because it leads to skills needed for advanced use. Read the information on the Cold War era to see how well you did with predicting/negotiating.

### Reading about the U.S. in the Cold War Era

In addition to increased economic power, the U.S. found itself in a new position of being a superpower involved in an East-West Cold War with the Soviet Union. Although no actual war with the U.S.S.R. (Union of Soviet Socialist Republics) existed, the arms race and the space race between the two countries led to the development of new weapons and **exploration** of outer space. While the goal of the U.S.S.R. was to spread **communism** throughout various areas of the world, the United States **declared** itself a supporter and promoter of **democracy.**

The importance of democracy as an ideal influenced both **domestic** and foreign activities in the 1950s and '60s that were aimed at ending communism—nicknamed the "red plague" by many U.S. Americans. These opposing ideals contributed to the Bay of Pigs Invasion in 1961—an unsuccessful attempt by the United States to overthrow the communist-influenced gov-

The White House stands as a symbol of democracy. (Courtesy DoD Visual Information Record Center.)

The Kremlin gate represented the ideals of communism. (Courtesy DoD Visual Information Record Center.)

ernment in nearby Cuba—and to the Cuban missile crisis in October 1962, a standoff between the United States and the Soviet Union that brought the world to the brink of nuclear war. The U.S. eventually agreed not to invade Cuba (and to remove missiles from Turkey) in exchange for the removal of Soviet missiles from Cuban soil.

This was the second wave of public **concern** about communism in twentieth century U.S. history. The first has become known as the era of "McCarthyism" at home. Joseph McCarthy was a U.S. senator from Wisconsin who led an anticommunist witch hunt in Washington, D.C., in the early fifties. He did this after Alger Hiss, a State Department official, was **accused** and found guilty of spying for the Soviets. This witch hunt was aimed at anyone and everyone who was thought to have ties to or **sympathies** for the

Communist Party and included many famous authors, playwrights, directors, and actors. The U.S. Communist Party was required to give a list of its members to the government, and those who had been **associated** with communism in other countries were not allowed to live in the United States. Communism was thought to be such a threat to the U.S. that neighbors and co-workers reported each other for **suspected** communist activities.

In other areas of the world, the United States **flooded** areas of Europe and Asia that were threatened by Soviet values with money and military aid in order to halt the spread of communism and to defend democracy where it existed. One example was the Marshall Plan, by which money was loaned to Western Europe to help with rebuilding after World War II. During one difficult winter, the U.S. flew food, blankets, and supplies to West Berlin so that the city did not fall to the **surrounding** Soviet occupation zone. All of this was **driven** by an idea called the "domino effect," or the belief that if one country fell to communism, the countries near it would fall also.

The U.S. **presence** in the Vietnam War was a result of concern over the domino effect. Vietnam was divided along political lines, with the North under Soviet and Chinese communist influence and the South wishing to remain democratic. Ideologically **bound** to help **struggling** South Vietnam, both President Dwight D. Eisenhower and President John F. Kennedy (JFK) sent "military advisors" to the area. By the time JFK was **assassinated** on November 22, 1963, more than 15,000 U.S. American soldiers were stationed in Vietnam. President Lyndon B. Johnson (LBJ), who became president after JFK's death, **extended** this effort by ordering U.S. forces to bomb the Northern Vietcong for attacks on U.S. ships off South Vietnam. The Tonkin Gulf Resolution passed by Congress in August 1964 gave the president the authority to act in Vietnam without officially declaring war. By March 1965, 184,000 U.S. American troops were fighting in Vietnam.

Much of the **population** did not support the U.S. actions in an Asian civil war, and war protests spread all across the nation, especially on college campuses. In 1970, at Kent State University in Ohio, four students were killed and several wounded when a few members of the National Guard shot into a crowd of protestors. As the president sent more soldiers to Vietnam and young men were **drafted** to fight, the protesting grew more and more **violent.** Many young men left for Canada, and others publicly burned draft cards and U.S. flags in the streets. In 1969, one hundred thousand people marched in Washington, D.C., to protest U.S. involvement in the war.

U.S. soldiers observe the Berlin Wall from the West German side, 1984. (Courtesy DoD Visual Information Record Center.)

A U.S. Army tank maneuvers in downtown Saigon, Vietnam, in 1966. (Courtesy DoD Visual Information Record Center.)

Visitors pay tribute at the Vietnam Veterans Memorial. (Courtesy DoD Visual Information Record Center.)

Building on public sentiment, Richard Nixon was elected president in 1968 by promising to end the war. (The U.S. would not officially leave Vietnam until 1975.) Because so many Americans were against the war, soldiers who fought in Vietnam came home to **scorn** and anger compared to the hero's welcome for soldiers of previous U.S. wars. The traumas these **veterans** experienced in Vietnam caused physical and emotional harm that left many unable to work. Homelessness among returning soldiers became a new social issue. In 1982, the U.S. government **recognized** the service of these veterans by building the Vietnam Veterans Memorial in Washington, D.C. Women veterans who served in Vietnam were honored with their own statue in 1993.

### Responding to Information about Defending Democracy from McCarthy to Vietnam

In the last two units, connections were made between the reading and your lives and between the reading and other texts. The last connection skill that is important is to be able to make connections between the reading and things going on in the world around us. These connections do not need to involve world powers or large countries. The events in the reading can remind us of things happening at our school, in our neighborhoods, or in our cities. Does some of the information in the reading remind you of things that are happening in the world? Write about it here.

### Understanding the Reading: Comprehension Check

This is a short answer comprehension check. All you need to do is briefly answer the questions in your own words.

1. Describe the kind of competition that took place between the United States and the Soviet Union during the Cold War.

2. Why did U.S. Americans call Communism the red plague?

3. What was McCarthyism? How did it relate to Communism?

4. How did the United States try to stop Communism from spreading in foreign countries?

5. Describe the domino effect.

6. How does the domino effect relate to the United States and the Vietnam War?

7. What differences are there in the way that Presidents Kennedy and Johnson responded to the crisis in Vietnam?

8. How did the population of the United States react to the involvement in Vietnam?

## Applying Our Understanding to Order Events in History

Using your knowledge of the progression of historical events before, during, and after the Vietnam War, put the following fourteen statements in the proper order.

___ Presidents Dwight D. Eisenhower and John F. Kennedy send "military advisors" to Vietnam to help South Vietnam remain stable.

___ Congress passes the Tonkin Gulf Resolution, allowing President Johnson to officially order bombing raids against North Vietnam.

___ Vietnam veterans are scorned and disrespected upon their return from the war.

___ Protesting at Kent State University in Ohio leaves four students dead and nine wounded.

— Richard M. Nixon is elected president of the United States.

— World War II ends, leaving two superpowers in the world with opposing economic systems and ideologies.

— The Vietnam Veterans Memorial is built and dedicated.

— The draft threatens many young men, and some leave the U.S. for Canada.

— 100,000 people march in Washington, D.C., to show the government what they think about the Vietnam conflict.

— The United States sends money and military aid to areas of the world threatened by communism.

— John F. Kennedy is assassinated. Vice President Lyndon B. Johnson is sworn in as president.

— A civil war erupts in Vietnam.

Now that you understand some important main points of information in the reading, let's apply that understanding to something outside of the textbook.

## Looking at a Poem from the Vietnam War Women's Memorial Project

The typical picture of the Vietnam veteran is of a young male. However, over a quarter of a million women also served voluntarily on the front lines of the war in military hospitals and offices. The difficulties that returning Vietnam soldiers encountered upon returning home made the Vietnam Memorial Wall a dream that was not publically realized until a decade after the end of the war. The Vietnam Women's Memorial was dedicated to honoring the sacrifices and service of the heroic women. This poem was written by a woman who was a nurse during the Vietnam War. Before you read the poem, think of a time when you chose not to think about something because it was too hard to deal with. What happened? Did not thinking about it help you or hurt you? Write about it here.

This poem, written by Dana Schuster in 1984, is about someone who put some memories away and then thought about them later. Choose a classmate to read the poem out loud and follow along as a class.

### Like Emily Dickinson

Like Emily Dickinson
tucking tight little poems
into corners and crannies
of her father's home
I tuck their names
into the crevices
of my crenelated heart.

Lonnie from Tennessee
smiling A-K amp [*arm amputee*]
"Don't mean nothin'.
I got another one"

Danny from LA
unable to see
the last dawn we shared

Chief the Ute
willing himself to die
since he could not
will himself to live
a partial man

Pocho from Arizona
who wanted only that
the last words he heard
be in his mother tongue
words rightfully spoken
by his mother who,
absent, became me

Skeets from somewhere
who asked me to sing
Amazing Grace
because his mother did

The boy with no name
no voice
no face

All these and more
I tuck away
later to peruse
perhaps edit
perhaps to erase
at some leisure time
at penance time
sometime in the future
that leaves them behind

Emily in white,
I in green,
we do our work
endure and abide
tucking away the hurt
saving it for a time
when alcoves need airing
when corners need cleaning
when hearts need healing
when there are no more
empty corners
convenient to fill

*Initial Reaction:* What emotions, memories, or ideas does the poem make you think of? Write about them here.

### Understanding Poetry and Figurative Meaning

Learning to guess the meaning of words in context is a good vocabulary skill. In verse 1, line 7 of the poem, Schuster writes of her *crenelated* heart. This is an uncommon word. Without looking in a dictionary, try to guess the meaning of the adjective *crenelated* based on the context of the overall meaning of the poem. Write down adjectives that you think may be similar in meaning here and compare with your classmates.

Look up *crenelated* in the dictionary and copy the definition here.

Who was closest?

Go through the rest of the poem and find unfamiliar vocabulary. Make a list of the words and follow the same process.

| Unfamiliar Word | What I Think it Means | Dictionary Definition |
|---|---|---|
|  |  |  |
|  |  |  |
|  |  |  |
|  |  |  |

*Literal Meaning:* Read the poem again, this time paying attention to some of the literal meaning and details of the words. Fill out the following chart about the six wounded men Schuster mentions. If you can't find it in the poem, write "no information."

| Name | Home State | Description |
|---|---|---|
| Lonnie | Tennessee | He has had an arm amputation. |
| | | |
| | | |
| | | |
| | | |
| | | |

*Figurative Meaning:* Poetry uses many different kinds of language to make meaning. This poem, like most poems, works with allusion, language register, and metaphors among other linguistic features. See if you can answer the following questions about the linguistic elements of the poem.

1. *Allusion* is information in a poem or piece of literature that refers to another person, place, event, or piece of work. Dana Schuster makes several allusions to the life and work of Emily Dickinson in the first and last verses of her poem.

---

**Emily Elizabeth Dickinson**
**1830–86**

Birth date: December 10, 1830
Birthplace: Amherst, Massachusetts
Education: Mount Holyoke Female Seminary
Biographical Data

- never married
- lived her whole life in her family home
- experienced anxiety and social withdrawal in her early 30s
- experienced a nervous breakdown in 1862
- spent most of her time at home writing, baking, and gardening
- wrote over 1800 poems; 10 published during her life

Nicknames: New England Mystic, Woman in White,
   Nun of Amherst
Died: May 15, 1886

---

Based on the information you have about Emily Dickinson, write comparisons between her and the poet Dana Schuster in the table below.

| Dana Schuster | Emily Dickinson |
|---|---|
| tucks names into her heart | tucks poems into the wall |
| | |
| | |
| | |

There is another allusion in the poem, not to a person, but to a text. Can you find it? Write it here.

2. *Language register* refers to the formality of language used. This is usually related to grammar and pronunciation. There is one example of a sentence in the poem with a change in register or formality. Can you find it? Write it here.

What effect does this sentence have on you as a reader?

Does the sentence make the poem more or less meaningful for you?

Why do you think Schuster decided to use that sentence in this poem?

3. A *metaphor* is an idea that is used symbolically in place of another. For example, this poem uses the metaphors of writing and of house-cleaning. Write words or phrases from the poem that go with each metaphor.

| Writing Metaphor | Housecleaning Metaphor |
|---|---|
|  |  |
|  |  |
|  |  |
|  |  |

*Final Reaction:* Read the poem again. What is the message that you got from the poem? What can you learn from it for your own everyday life?

## Using a Cinquain Poetry Format to Write Our Own Poems in English

Writing for ourselves is a great way to release stress, practice English, and be creative. Cinquain is an American poetry form influenced by Japanese haiku that has five lines.

Cinquain Poetry

Line one: State the subject in one word (usually a noun).
Line two: Describe the subject in two words (often noun + adjective or adjective + adjective).
Line three: Describe some action about the noun in three words.
Line four: Express an emotion about the subject in four words.
Line five: Restate the subject in another single word or title that reflects what has already been said. (usually a noun)

Here is a cinquain poem about Vietnam nurses.

woman
vulnerable polarity
creating, protecting, defending
rock solid, glass fragile
Vietnam nurse

Try your own cinquain poem on war, personal memories, or another topic that interests you.

**Link to Today**

## Campus ROTC—Who Are Those Students in Uniform?

You might have seen them early one cold morning on campus, lined up in uniform standing at attention or exercising. They are U.S. citizens and fellow students who are there to learn about life, customs, and career choices in the U.S. military and to earn a little extra money for school. Freshman and sophomore students are "trying on" the military for size. There is no obligation for them to be there; rather, they are finding out whether this is something they might want to pursue as a career in the future. Juniors, seniors, and even some graduate students who participate have made a four- to ten-year commitment to the U.S. military and will enter as officers when they graduate from school. They are eligible to receive scholarships and a tax-free, monthly stipend while they participate.

Another option to earn money for college is to serve for four or more years in the military prior to pursuing postsecondary education. Funds for college tuition are available through a law called the *Montgomery GI Bill*. This education program has been available to returning servicemen and women since World War II to help veterans further their training and education in civilian fields. Many students on campus are recipients of this money, but because they are no longer active-duty military personnel, you will be very unlikely to recognize them.

## Fast Facts

- According to a 2000 statement by the Department of Veterans Affairs, half of all service members who qualify for *Montgomery GI Bill* money for school did not use it.

- Recruiting and retaining skilled people has become a challenge for the U.S. military in a tight job market.

- The Pentagon estimates that over two thousand public high schools do not allow military recruiters on campus.

### Positive Aspects of Military Service
Find and read a newspaper, magazine, or Internet article on a positive aspect of military service. Summarize it in your own words.

### Negative Aspects of Military Service
Find and read a newspaper, magazine, or Internet article on a negative aspect of military service. Summarize it in your own words.

### My Personal Conclusion(s) about Higher Education and the Military in the United States

## Putting It All Together

Think about what you have learned in this unit and from the activities you did. Write down your ideas about these questions. Then, in groups of three, talk about them and other questions or observations you might have.

1. What surprised me the most about information on the Cold War era in the United States?

2. What does this information help me to understand about life in the United States?

3. How does knowing this information change my mind about U.S. American values and attitudes?

4. Can people learn something from the experiences U.S. Americans had with the Cold War, McCarthyism, and the Vietnam War?

5. What will I tell people now if they ask me about democracy in the United States?

6. What kinds of positive changes can be made regarding decisions to fight wars?

# 7 The U.S. in the Seventies

## Women, the Feminist Movement, and the ERA

Young feminists transform a statue into a living testament of their power and strength, 1997. (Photo by Susan Mackenzie.)

## Net Surfers

See what information you can find by searching for the following names, words, and phrases on the World Wide Web.

| | |
|---|---|
| Equal Rights Amendment | National Women's Hall of Fame |
| Future Homemakers of America | National Women's History Project |
| Homemaking | Planned Parenthood |
| Ms. Foundation for Women | Title IX |

## Presidential Suite

Lyndon B. Johnson (D) 1963–69
Richard M. Nixon (R) 1969–74
Gerald R. Ford (R) 1974–77
James Earl (Jimmy) Carter, Jr. (D) 1977–81

## On TV

*The Mary Tyler Moore Show*
*That '70s Show*

## Music Box

"I Am Woman" - Helen Reddy
"9 to 5" - Dolly Parton

## At the Movies

*When Billie Beat Bobby*
*9 to 5*

### Preparing to Read about Women, the Feminist Movement, and the ERA

You can probably tell by looking at the title that this unit is going to be a continuation of some of the same kinds of issues brought up in previous chapters. Even though this chapter overlaps with the events surrounding equal rights in Unit 4 and the Vietnam War in Unit 6, we will now turn our attention to the homefront again. While the U.S. was involved in problems related to political ideologies overseas, there were still people living in this country who were not satisfied with social ideologies regarding women. The feminist seeds planted during the civil rights movement of the 1960s blossomed in the 1970s. Unfortunately, the outcome of these events is a little disappointing, but the importance of the feminist movement in the United States is still being felt today. Once again, start by interviewing a classmate. Ask for the following information

> about women's rights
>> the legal rights/obligations of women
>> the social expectations of women and their roles in society in his/her community
>> the personal opinion he/she has about the rights/obligations of women

> about child care
>> the type and availability of child-care for working women in his/her community
>> the public opinion about stay-at-home vs. working mothers in his/her community
>> the personal opinion he/she has about who should take care of and raise children

> about abortion
>> the laws regarding abortion
>> the public opinion about abortion in his/her community
>> the personal thoughts he/she has about abortion

As always, you should never feel obligated to share information that is too personal with your classmates. Narrating and listening to different ideas, experiences, and opinions is a great way to lay the foundations for the kind of opinion sharing and hypothesis formation that characterizes advanced English usage though, so it is a helpful activity to engage in as much as you are able. Showing respect for others' ideas and experiences is also an important skill to gain. It is a skill that is valued very much in the United States and sharing ideas about controversial issues provides a good place to practice showing respect for diversity through language. (We'll focus on diversity in the U.S. in the last unit.)

For now, have a classmate list the issues you discussed on the board. Then as a class, summarize what you have learned from each other and have the classmate jot these ideas down on the board. There should be many different experiences and ideas to discuss.

## Learning New Vocabulary about the U.S. in the Seventies

**availability (n)** existence of and access to something

**decade (n)** ten-year time period

**form of address (n)** a title given to a person and used to show respect (or disrespect); common forms of address in U.S. American English are: Mr., Mrs., Miss, Ms., Dr., etc. (These are sometimes called *honorifics*.) Still common in formal writing, honorifics (particularly those signaling marital status) are used less often in speech today.

**representation (n)** a voice for the concerns of a group

**thesis (n)** the main argument of a piece of writing

**trend (n)** a situation that grows more and more popular

**workforce (n)** all employed people

**to be caught up in (v)** to be in the middle of or heavily involved in something

**to coin (v)** to create a new word or term in a language

**to ensure (v)** to make sure that something exists

**to fall short (v)** to not make a goal or not have enough; to be inadequate

**to launch (v)** to begin; to introduce a product to the market

**to organize (v)** to plan an event or lead a group of people in a movement or activity

**to ratify (v)** to approve; in the U.S. government, the act of individual state representatives voting to pass new amendments to the U.S. Constitution (those already passed in Congress)

**to swell (v)** to grow large

**affordable (adj)** reasonably priced so that most people can buy it

**characteristic (adj)** setting apart a person, event, or time period

**currently (adv)** now; at this time

**disappointed (adj)** losing hope or expectation; let down

**landmark (adj)** marking an important event or turning point in history

**unfulfilled (adj)** unhappy; a concept or person not reaching its true potential

### Talking about New Words and Ideas

Use your understanding of the new vocabulary words to discuss the following questions with a partner or in a group.

1. To **coin** a new word is the process of making up new words for new ideas that people think of. This is the way language changes to fit the changing needs of its users. Often, new words are invented by the young and then spread to the mainstream population. When a word is put into the dictionary, it becomes part of the standard language of that country. Of course, by that time, many other new words have come into use by the young.

   A. What new words have entered your native language since you were a child?
   B. How did different people of different age groups react to the word(s)? Why do you think this happened?
   C. Do you think that the creation of new words changes society, or does a changing society create new words? Give one example to support your opinion.
   D. How does the creation of new words affect you as you learn English?
   E. List any words that are related to the verb **coin** in your mind.

2. Languages have different patterns of addressing people and showing the relationship/distance between two or more speakers. Many languages have a formal and an informal *you* form. Some languages use different vocabulary or word endings depending on the age, social distance, and respect of the speakers involved. Most languages rely on a combination of these elements. Other languages such as English rely mostly on **forms of address** (linguists refer to these as *honorifics*). For example, Mr. William Jones can be called in polite/distanced speech *Mr. Jones* or in informal/close speech *William* or in family/friend speech *Will* or *Bill*. How do speakers of your native language show respect/disrespect to the people they are speaking with?

   A. Do you think there is a relationship between the way different languages show respect and the way relationships between various people function in different societies? Give examples from your native language and other languages you know.
   B. Can you think of ways that people can use patterns of addressing people as tools to show equality? Dominance? Subordination? To make social change?
   C. How important do you think it is to be familiar with various forms of address in the country of the language you are learning?
   D. List any words that are related to **form of address** in your mind.

3. In U.S. American writing patterns, a **thesis** is considered to be the most important part of the writing assignment. If you are planning to write for a U.S. American audience, it is expected that the thesis, or a summary of the main points of the argument, is clear and easy to find. A thesis statement is generally expected to be seen in the first paragraph of a short paper and relatively close to the beginning of a longer paper. This is a cultural pattern that reflects the expectation of the U.S. American reader. It is no better or worse than any other way to organize information, but being aware of and using it correctly is important if you want to be understood by a U.S. American audience.

   A. Where does the main idea appear in writing in your native language? Compare this to your classmates.

B. Think of a book or an article you read recently (in any language). Can you summarize the main argument of the book in a one-sentence thesis?

C. List any words that are related to **thesis** in your mind.

4. When there is not enough of something to reach a goal, we say that the effort **falls short.** This can be used concretely, as in money or resources, or it can be used abstractly in the sense of something does not reach its full potential, such as an idea or a plan.

A. Can you think of a time in your life when you or an effort you were involved in fell short?

B. How did it make you feel? Did you try again?

C. If something is important to the people, such as passing a new law, how important is it for them to keep trying? Why?

D. Can efforts that fall short still be important in a country's history, even if they do not succeed?

E. List any words that are related to **falling short** in your mind.

5. An important event in a nation or an organization's history is called a **landmark** event. In this case, it is used as an adjective to describe the event. It may help you to know that as a noun, a landmark also refers to a famous place. Both refer to something out of the ordinary or special which people use to mark a place in space or time.

A. What are some landmark events in your country's history? Explain their importance.

B. What are some landmark events in your personal life? Explain their importance.

C. List any words that are related to **landmark** in your mind.

## Making Predictions about the Reading

Without looking at the reading, and based on the interviews and new vocabulary words, make a list of five ideas you expect to show up in the reading. Next to your idea, write down a reason why you think each idea will be included. It can be based on anything you have seen in the unit (photos, text, etc.) so far, and there is no right or wrong answer. This activity involves making a hypothesis (a reasonable guess) and supporting an opinion—two indicators of advanced English usage. It also involves looking for evidence in the unit to support your opinion—an important college-level writing skill.

1.

Because

2.

Because

3.

Because

4.

Because

5.

Because

Let's see how you did with your predictions.

## Reading about the U.S. in the Seventies

At the beginning of the 1970s, the United States was **caught up** in violent protests against the still-raging Vietnam War and feeling the effects of continued racism despite the civil rights movement of the previous **decade.** New concerns about an energy crisis and about protecting the environment added to these worries. In the middle of all this, women were busy **organizing** to claim the full benefits of rights that they fought for during the suffrage movement in the 1920s and that had seemed to take a back seat to the issues of war and economy **characteristic** of post–World War II America.

Although women in the United States fought for and won the right to vote in 1920, they still faced discrimination in many areas of their lives. In 1950, 18.4 million women worked outside of the home. Continuing a growing **trend** since World War II and influenced by psychologist Betty Friedan's book *The Feminist Mystique*° in the 1960s, these numbers **swelled** over

---

° *The Feminist Mystique* was based on in-depth interviews and statistical analyses of information obtained in research on U.S. American housewives. Its main **thesis** was that women were bored, frustrated,

Women march for their beliefs during the Young Feminist Summit in 1997. (Photo by Susan Mackenzie.)

time. However, statistics showed that those women were earning 58.2% of a man's salary for doing the same type of work. **Currently,** there are over 63 million women in the **workforce,** but the average salary has only grown to 76 cents for every dollar earned by a man. Other issues of growing concern for women involved in the Feminist Movement during the 1970s were equal access to educational and economic loans, the **representation** of women in politics, the **availability** of legal abortion, and the right to control their own lives.

In 1970, to mark the fiftieth anniversary of the suffrage movement and the constitutional right to vote, marches were organized in support of the Equal Rights Amendment (ERA), an amendment to the Constitution. This amendment was originally proposed during the suffrage movement and made discrimination on the basis of sex and unequal pay illegal, **insuring** equal opportunities in all states by federal law. In 1972, journalists Gloria

and **unfulfilled** as housewives. Friedan's proposed solution to these findings was more opportunity for women to work outside the home to help them with self-discovery and a better understanding of their own identity. Many viewed these ideas as a threat to the family and the right of women to be valued as wives and mothers.

Steinem and Letty Cottin Pogrebin **launched** *Ms.*\*\*—a feminist magazine—to keep women informed on the issues affecting their lives. (*Ms.* is still published today.)

In 1973, the U.S. Supreme Court reached a **landmark** decision in the case of *Roe* v. *Wade,* making it illegal for any individual state to deny women the right to obtain a legal abortion during the first three months of pregnancy. For many this decision has come to represent equality for women in the United States. However, there is also a vocal opposition to this decision, making abortion rights one of the most hotly debated issues on the public agenda today. Also in 1973, Billie Jean King contributed to the feminist cause by challenging Bobby Riggs, a male player, to a tennis match and then winning. In 1977, the First National Women's Conference was held to involve the U.S. Congress in creating jobs for all women who wanted to work, and to improve the availability of **affordable,** quality child care. Leaders of the feminist movement were **disappointed** when, after ten years of debate, the Equal Rights Amendment failed to be **ratified** in 1982, **falling short** of the needed number of votes by three states.

## Responding to Information about Women, the Feminist Movement, and the ERA

Fill in the first blank of each sentence with an adjective that describes your feeling or opinion and then finish the sentence. The first one has been done for you.

1. I think discrimination in the workplace is *unfair* because *there are many talented working women.*

2. I think an Equal Rights Amendment is _____ because _____

_____ .

3. I think *Roe* v. *Wade* is _____ because _____

_____ .

---

\*\**Ms.* Magazine is a feminist publication dedicated to expanding awareness of the female self and feminism. *Ms.* is a relatively new **form of address** in U.S. American English. It is a combination of *Mrs.* and *Miss* titles, which show marital status and are linked to age/respect. *Ms.* was **coined** as a form of address because men's marital status is not indicated by *Mr.*, and many thought that there should be a similar form for women who did not want their marital status to be the first thing people knew about them.

4. I think *The Feminist Mystique* is _____ because _____

_____ .

5. I think the honorifics/forms of address are _____ because \_\_

_____ .

### Understanding the Reading: Comprehension Check

One way to know if you have understood something that you have read is to be able to retell it in your own words. Write a short letter to an English-speaking friend or classmate, narrating and describing what you learned from the reading. Don't worry about using the same order of events or the same words as the reading does, as this is not a memorization task. Just rewrite the information the way you understand it. You may write your own thoughts and opinions if you want to, but save it for the last paragraph so it doesn't get confused with the information from the reading.

### Applying What We Know: Taking a Gender-Sensitivity Assessment

Use the following survey to assess your and your classmates' gender sensitivity.

|  | Always | Often | Sometimes | Rarely | Never |
|---|---|---|---|---|---|
| 1. I refer to men and women by their appropriate social/academic/ professional titles. |  |  |  |  |  |
| 2. I give proper credit to men and women who contribute to projects I am involved in. |  |  |  |  |  |

| | Always | Often | Sometimes | Rarely | Never |
|---|---|---|---|---|---|
| 3. I look for opportunities to spend time interacting with both males and females. | | | | | |
| 4. I avoid judging men and women by social stereotypes, giving each individual the opportunity to be their own person. | | | | | |
| 5. I avoid sexist language such as exclusive use of male pronouns when speaking and writing in English. | | | | | |
| 6. I do not allow others to tell sexist jokes about men or women in my presence. | | | | | |
| 7. I take the advice of female professionals (such as doctors or professors) just as seriously as that of male professionals. | | | | | |
| 8. I bring up gender as a discussion topic with my friends, family, and classmates. | | | | | |
| 9. I respond seriously and thoughtfully to ideas brought up by both men and women in class or in conversations. | | | | | |
| 10. I support both men and women in achieving their dreams and goals. | | | | | |

Were there items on the survey that you had never thought about before? In which column were most of your responses?

Now that you understand and can rewrite information about the feminist movement in your own words, let's look at what a U.S. American sports legend and promoter of women's rights has said.

## Looking at an Autobiography: *Billie Jean* by Tennis Star Billie Jean King

In the following paragraphs from her 1974 autobiography, Billie Jean King describes an encounter with an admirer and her feelings about it.

> A strange thing happened back at the Auditorium after I'd finished a light workout. A woman in her early thirties with this odd, intense look in her eyes— she was almost crying—grabbed me by the shoulders and almost before I could say a word told me how she'd been forced to give up athletics when she was a teenager because of pressure from her family. She said she felt foolish even talking to me, but that I was the only idol she'd ever had in her life and she was glad that women finally had somebody of their own sex they could look up to.
>
> I didn't know how to answer, I really didn't. I don't even know if she expected an answer. This kind of thing has happened more and more over the last couple of years and I'm always taken aback when it does. It confuses and embarrasses me because I guess I don't really understand what kind of impact I, or my tennis, or my success, or whatever it is, has on other women. But it sure means something to them. Maybe because I've been successful I sometimes forget how tough it is for women to even have the opportunity to succeed. . . .
>
> Larry [Larry King, Billie Jean's husband] and I got off on a discussion about the lousy deal girls are still getting in interscholastic sports, something that he and I have talked a lot about lately. It's unbelievable. In 1971 there were 300,000 girls in the entire country in high school sports; in 1973 there were 800,000. Quite a jump until you remember how small the base figure is. . . . Won't there still be lots of frustrated women like the one who talked to me . . . ? (9–13)

## Writing Our Own Brief Autobiographies

Autobiographies contain a person's life story written in first person. Biography is the story of a person's life written by another person. The information you read about Emily Dickinson in the last unit is an example of biographical information. An autobiography has information about your birth, early childhood, and memorable educational or developmental experiences. It also usually contains some reflection on these experiences. Write a summary of your life, including some reflection on what makes you who you are today. You will be giving this information to a classmate for the next exercise, so be sure not to include anything that you want to remain private.

## Using Quoted vs. Reported Speech to Talk about the Experiences of Others

Representing our own experiences is an important language skill. However, it is also important to know how to represent the experiences of others. In writing, this is accomplished in one of two ways: using direct quotes, or using reported speech. In speaking, reported speech is used exclusively. Look at the difference between direct speech and indirect speech.

| Quoted/Direct Speech | Reported/Indirect Speech |
| --- | --- |
| Billie Jean King said, "It confuses and embarrasses me because I guess I don't really understand what kind of impact I, or my tennis, or my success has on other women." <br><br> • first person pronouns (*I, we*) <br> • said, ". . ." <br> • various tenses | Billie Jean King *said that she was confused* and *embarrassed* because she *didn't* really understand what kind of impact she, or her tennis, or her success, *had* on other women. <br><br> • third person pronouns (*he, she, they*) <br> • said that <br> • past tense forms |

Work together with a classmate. Exchange autobiographies and write five direct quotes from them. Then, change the quotes into indirect speech.

| Wendy wrote, "I am an ESL teacher." | Wendy wrote that she was an ESL teacher. |
| --- | --- |
| 1. | |
| 2. | |
| 3. | |
| 4. | |
| 5. | |

## Applying our Knowledge of Reported Speech to Academic Skills: Paraphrasing and Summarizing

Paraphrasing and summarizing ideas are important intermediate-level language skills. *Paraphrasing* is another name for using reported or indirect speech. A good summary is usually about 15–20% of the length of the original text. Summarizing and paraphrasing usually go hand in hand because using reported speech effectively shortens a text and preserves the main ideas. The sample from Billie Jean King's autobiography was about 250 words long. This 50-word summary is 20% of the length of the original text.

> Billie Jean wrote that a woman spoke with her and said that she had been forced to give up sports. The woman said that she was glad women had someone to be a role model. Billie Jean wrote that she was embarrassed and that she didn't understand the impact she had on other women.

Summarize your classmate's autobiography by using indirect speech.

**Link to Today**

## Take Our Daughters to Work Day— What Is the Future for Girls?

Every year since 1993, on the fourth Thursday in April, American girls between the ages of 9 and 15 are invited to go to work with a parent, friend, or mentor. The program is sponsored by the Ms. Foundation for Women and is designed to let young girls see how valuable women's contributions are to the economy and the workplace. The program was designed to help girls be confident in themselves and their abilities, to help them find role models, and to help them plan for their futures, especially in traditionally male-dominated fields. Look at the following information about Take Our Daughters to Work Day and other similar activities that have grown from it, such as Daughters on Campus Day.

A Ms. Foundation advertising campaign for Take Our Daughters to Work Day

## Fast Facts

- The Ms. Foundation estimates that 19 million girls went to work with a parent on Take Our Daughters to Work Day 1999.

- Many U.S. companies open the event to both boys and girls.

- Especially for Boys is a classroom curriculum designed to keep boys in school and away from the workplace on Take Our Daughters to Work Day.

- Conservative women's groups claim that Take Our Daughters to Work Day creates bias against the home and the family. Others criticize it as a corporate "window dressing" highlighting white-collar work and ignoring low-paying and dangerous jobs.

- Many parents and teachers are asking to have Take Our Daughters to Work Day moved from the fourth Thursday in April to a summer day, stating that missing a day of school disrupts learning.

**Positive Aspects of Take Our Daughters to Work Day**
Find and read a newspaper, magazine, or Internet article on a positive aspect of taking children to work. Summarize it in your own words.

**Negative Aspects of Take Our Daughters to Work Day**
Find and read a newspaper, magazine, or Internet article on a negative aspect of taking children to work. Summarize it in your own words.

**My Personal Conclusion(s) About Take Our Daughters to Work Day**

Can you make any predictions based on this information? Imagine what Take Our Daughters to Work Day or Daughters on Campus Day will be like in the year 2050. Write a headline or create a banner for it here:

## Putting It All Together

Think about what you have learned in this unit. First, take some quiet time to reflect on and write down your ideas about the feminist movement. Make connections between ideas as they come to you. Then, think about and make notes on your responses to these questions. When you are finished, discuss them in groups of three. Where do most people agree? Are there differences in the way people think? Compare and contrast your answers with the group. Then, present your results to the class.

1. What surprised me most about the feminist movement and the proposed Equal Rights Amendment?

2. How does this information about the feminist movement and the proposed Equal Rights Amendment help me understand modern U.S. American life?

3. How does knowing this information change my mind/reinforce my beliefs about U.S. American values and attitudes?

4. Can people in my community learn something from the lessons that the United States took from the feminist movement and the proposed Equal Rights Amendment?

5. What will I tell people now if they ask me about the status of women in the United States?

6. What kinds of positive changes can my community make regarding the role and status of women? Should it make any changes at all?

# 8 The U.S. as It Looks toward the 21st Century

## Diversity vs. Unity in the New Millennium

Tucson Human Freedom Flag—Residents of Tucson, Arizona, form a human flag on a baseball field to raise money for the Red Cross after the September 11, 2001, terrorist attacks. (Photo courtesy Nancy DeMille.)

## Net Surfers

See what information you can find by searching for the following names, words, and phrases on the World Wide Web.

American Civil Liberties Union       Hate crime legislation

Christian Coalition                         Liberal views and ideas

Conservative views and ideas        Moral Majority

Equal access

---

### *Presidential Suite*

James Earl (Jimmy) Carter, Jr. (D) 1977–81
Ronald W. Reagan (R) 1981–89
George H. W. Bush (R) 1989–93
William (Bill) J. Clinton (D) 1993–2001
George W. Bush (R) 2001–

---

### Preparing to Read about Diversity vs. Unity in the New Millennium

U.S. American history in the last two decades of the 20th century is a series of rapid ups and downs, twists and turns, and major changes right up to and continuing into the 21st century. Find a classmate to work with and ask

about hate crimes
> the kind of hate crimes that have been/are being committed in your classmate's community
> the laws, if any, regarding hate crimes in his/her community
> the personal experiences he/she has had with hate crimes, if any

about diversity
> the kinds of religious, ethnic, social, or other diversity that exist in his/her community
> the government's role, if any, in protecting or promoting diversity in his/her community
> the general public opinion about promoting diversity in his/her community

about national unity

    the importance of national unity

    the kinds of activities that he/she feels preserve national unity

    the public perception of whether his/her country is unified or not

As has been the case in previous units, you should never feel that you must share information that is too personal. You are already familiar with the reasons why sharing information is helpful to successful language learning, so take this last opportunity to discuss as a class what you have learned about/from each other.

## Learning New Vocabulary about the U.S. as It Looks toward the 21st Century

**brutality (n)** the act of being cruel or violent; the use of excessive harmful physical force

**climate (n)** in this case, condition or set of attitudes about the events one is surrounded by

**conservatism (n)** a philosophy or belief that likes tradition and opposes change

**discourse (n)** a large-scale, public-level discussion about or representation of something

**diversity (n)** representing many differences

**echo (n)** in this case, something left over from or caused by the past

**focus (n)** the main thing that is paid attention to

**harassment (n)** mistreating someone through annoyance, threats, or demands

**liberalism (n)** a philosophy or attitude that is generally opposed to tradition and favors change toward a freer or less restricted society

**status (n)** position relative to others

**term (n)** in this case, a period of time; a presidential term lasts for four years and a president is allowed to serve for two terms or a total of eight years

**weapons (n)** instruments used for war or violence, such as guns or bombs

**to appoint (v)** to put somebody in a position, usually one of leadership

**to maintain (v)** to keep something in its original state

**to overcome (v)** to succeed despite difficulty

**to promote (v)** to speak for something; to advance it publically

**to remain (v)** to stay or be left over from an earlier time

**to respect (v)** to feel or show regard for

**to restore (v)** to put something back into its original state or position

**to widen (v)** to get bigger and bigger across; to make the space between two things larger

**to worsen (v)** to become more of a problem

**varied (adj)** having a lot of variety or difference

## Talking about New Words and Ideas

1. When someone uses excessive physical force against someone else, it is referred to as **brutality.** Many U.S. Americans are concerned about the level of police brutality. Have there ever been instances of police brutality in your community? Describe what you know about it.

   A. Is there an official policy on police brutality in your community? What is it?
   B. Is police brutality justifiable in some cases? When do you think it is OK for police officers to use force? When is it not OK?
   C. List any words that are related to **brutality** in your mind.

2. The word **climate** usually refers to the weather. For example, the desert has a dry climate. The word can also refer to your surroundings in general. U.S. Americans often talk about the political climate when discussing events going on around them that have an effect on the feel of their everyday lives. For example, the Cold War climate of the 1950s and 1960s made U.S. Americans feel uneasy and unsettled, whereas the climate of economic boom in the 1990s tended to make people feel more secure. However, since the

terrorist attacks of September 11, 2001, the climate can be described as jittery or tense.

A.  How would you describe the current political climate in places you have lived or are living? What are the reasons for this climate? How does it make people feel?
B.  Is there anything that could make this climate change rapidly? If so, what?
C.  Do you feel comfortable with the current political climate you find yourself in? Why or why not?
D.  List any words that are related to the political use of the word **climate** in your mind.

3.  An attitude of opposition toward liberal trends and increased diversity in society is generally labeled **conservatism.** Although this attitude can be found in U.S. citizens from all walks of life, it tends to show up in groups of people who are wealthier than average, Caucasian, and/or fundamentally religious. One interesting cultural/political dynamic to note is that such people tend to be attracted to the beliefs of the Republican Party, although this is changing somewhat as the agendas of both parties become more and more similar as time progresses.

A.  Is there a distinct opposition between conservatism and liberalism in your community? If so, who belongs to each of these groups and what issues are they dealing with?
B.  Do you think that people who subscribe to conservatism have something to gain from it? What? How about people who subscribe to liberalism?
C.  What is to be lost by those who hold exclusively to either one of these viewpoints?
D.  List any words that are related to **conservatism** in your mind.

4.  Everything that is circulated in public or in private about an issue is referred to in a broad sense as **discourse.** This can include written and spoken language as well as images and metaphors, among others. Discourse is important because it feeds public opinion about people

and issues. Discourse can be manipulated to create public regard for certain issues.

A. What discourse(s) is/are currently important in your community? Who shapes this/these discourse(s). Why do they shape it/them in such a manner?

B. What kinds of negative discourses do you notice in your own community? Positive ones?

C. What effect can the public have on changing harmful discourses or promoting positive ones? What effect can you have personally?

D. List any words that are related to **discourse** in your mind.

5. When somebody excessively annoys, threatens, or makes demands of somebody we refer to it as **harassment.** There are many types of harassment, but one of the most talked-about forms is sexual harassment in the workplace. This refers to a work environment in which women are subjected to a range of problems from men making comments about their bodies or posting sexually explicit materials to men demanding sexual favors from women as requisite for women keeping their jobs or asking for sexual advances to be returned in exchange for promotions. This kind of harassment also happens toward men in some environments, but is less documented. Efforts to legislate protections against workplace harassment and to prosecute offenders in the U.S. have increased dramatically in recent times.

A. What kinds of harassment exist in the workplace in your community? What effect do you think that it has on the workers and in the workplace?

B. Are there any specific laws about or against harassment? If so, what are they and how well are they enforced?

C. Have you ever experienced harassment personally? If so, in what context? Were you able to do anything to stop the harassment?

D. List any words that are related to **harassment** in your mind.

## Making Predictions about the Reading

Now that you have begun to learn historical and cultural information, you will probably be reading more and more informative and interesting things about the history and culture of the United States in the future. Since this is the last predicting that we will be doing together, let's go all out. First, make your list of five things you think will be in the reading. Then, compare with another person and agree. Then double the group size every time, to four, then eight, etc., until the entire class negotiates and agrees on the five main points they expect to see. During this process, keep in mind the cultural importance of respect and politeness when discussing different viewpoints. When everybody is satisfied, check your answers against the reading.

## Reading about the U.S. as It Looks toward the 21st Century

The internal and external forces that carried the United States to the dawn of the 21st century are **varied** and complex. While the population changed from within, the world around the U.S. changed too, leaving U.S. Americans to **adjust** to changes in the nation's identity. The **echoes** of the civil rights and feminist movements brought increased **status** for women and minorities during the 1980s. It was during this decade that a woman was appointed to the Supreme Court, Sandra Day O'Connor, and a woman astronaut, Sally Ride, was launched into space. President Ronald Reagan signed legislation making Martin Luther King, Jr., Day a federal holiday. The gay pride movement, which started in the sixties and seventies, became stronger in a **climate** of increased attention to **diversity.** In reaction to these trends, a public force calling itself the Moral Majority became vocal in its attempts to **restore** and promote **conservatism** in U.S. American public life. Although this group broke up in 1981, there are many who continue to **promote** the conservative values of the traditional home and family as the basis of U.S. society.

Economic problems and conflict with the Middle East **remaining** from the time of Jimmy Carter's presidency added to an overall sense of fear as

Sally Ride is launched into space on the space shuttle in 1983. (Courtesy DoD Visual Information Record Center.)

the Cold War with the Soviet Bloc dragged on and peaked during Ronald Reagan's presidency. **Weapons** agreements, summit talks, and a missile space shield proposal (nicknamed "Star Wars" by the public) characterized Reagan's two **terms** as president. The **worsening** domestic economic crisis left a **widening** gap between the wealthy and the poor. The fading American dream became a nightmare for the growing number of homeless and unemployed.

But then suddenly, the Cold War ended with the fall of the Berlin Wall in 1989, leaving the United States in the somewhat odd position of being the only superpower. In addition to this external factor, the economy began to improve in the 1990s. While external relations were heavily **focused** on the Middle Eastern Gulf War in the early nineties, attentions at home were centered on public **discourses** on several different topics. Sexual **harassment** was the central issue of the highly publicized Anita Hill and Clarence Thomas hearings. Racism and police **brutality** was illustrated by the Rodney King case, the riots in Los Angeles, and the Louima case in New York City. Hate crimes received wide attention after the beating death of gay college student Matthew Shepard in Wyoming. Questions about the legality and practicality of the U.S. electoral process were highlighted by the historic problems of the 2000 presidential election between Al Gore and George W. Bush.

**Respecting** individual personal freedoms guaranteed by the U.S. Constitution, protecting diversity, and **overcoming** a wide split in public opinion while **maintaining** a sense of national unity seem to be among the greatest domestic challenges for the United States today. This sense of unity was tested on September 11, 2001, when four U.S. airliners

A West German girl and an East German guard talk to each other through the recently opened Berlin Wall—a symbol for the end of the Cold War.

New York City firefighters walk past the U.S. flag after the September 11 attack on the World Trade Center. (U.S. Naval photo.)

were hijacked by terrorists. Two of them were flown into the Twin Towers of the World Trade Center in New York City, one into the Pentagon, and one crashed in Pennsylvania. These events had a tremendous effect on the country's view of itself and its place in the world. The response to these events both politically and personally from a wide spectrum of U.S. citizens perhaps hints at the spirit of the United States as it enters the new century.

### Responding to Information about Diversity vs. Unity in the New Millennium

You have taken a century-long journey with the people and the history of the United States. Based on what you have learned about the last 100 years, make predictions and complete the following sentences about the United States in the year 2100. There are no right or wrong answers. Just use your knowledge and your imagination.

In the year 2100, the American Dream will mean . . .

In the year 2100, the relationship between the United States and Russia will best be described as . . .

In the year 2100, the relationship between the United States and the Middle East will best be described as . . .

In the year 2100, feminism in the United States will be . . .

In the year 2100, the United States will elect its presidents by . . .

In the year 2100, conservative attitudes will be . . .

In the year 2100, liberal attitudes will be . . .

In the year 2100, racism in the United States will be . . .

In the year 2100, life in the United States of America will be . . .

## Understanding the Reading: Comprehension Check

Retelling information from reading is probably one of the most difficult skills to learn in a foreign language. Without looking back, take a few moments to jot down some notes from the reading in your own words. Then, with your books closed, retell the information to a classmate as you understand it and in your own words.

## Applying What We've Learned about Diversity: Assessing Sensitivity

Use the survey to gauge your and your classmates' sensitivity to diversity on campus.

|  | Always | Usually | Sometimes | Rarely | Never |
|---|---|---|---|---|---|
| 1. I look for opportunities to spend time with other students from different countries. |  |  |  |  |  |
| 2. I speak out against stereotypes and stereotyping in class and on campus. |  |  |  |  |  |
| 3. I bring up diversity as a conversation topic with my friends or classmates. |  |  |  |  |  |
| 4. If I notice discrimination happening around me, I say something about it. |  |  |  |  |  |
| 5. I encourage others not to speak badly of other races, religions, or cultures. |  |  |  |  |  |

|  | Always | Usually | Sometimes | Rarely | Never |
|---|---|---|---|---|---|
| 6. I choose topics related to diversity for class projects and research. |  |  |  |  |  |
| 7. I point out positive characteristics if people complain about others. |  |  |  |  |  |
| 8. I keep an open mind towards others' thoughts, beliefs, attitudes and emotions. |  |  |  |  |  |
| 9. I make myself familiar with the cultural practices of various community groups. |  |  |  |  |  |
| 10. I am aware of my own prejudices and consciously avoid acting on them. |  |  |  |  |  |

How did you do on the diversity assessment? Use your new knowledge of diversity issues in the United States to help you understand a recent debate about public art.

## The FDR Wheelchair Statue: Looking at a Sculpture from a U.S. Memorial

The way that a country chooses to immortalize its heroes is an important indicator of public values and beliefs. Washington, D.C., has many memorials and monuments to former presidents such as George Washington, Abraham Lincoln, Thomas Jefferson, and John F. Kennedy. In 1997, a new U.S. memorial to Franklin D. Roosevelt (FDR) was dedicated. One feature of the memorial is a statue of President Roosevelt sitting in a chair draped with a cape. The cape was designed by the artist to hide something that FDR painstakingly hid during his presidency at midcentury—the wheelchair he often relied on as the effects of polio worsened throughout his life.

Franklin D. Roosevelt statue at the FDR Memorial. (Photo courtesy Don Ward.)

When the tribute to FDR was being designed, disability advocates asked for an additional statue showing FDR in a wheelchair. It was from his wheelchair that Roosevelt led the country out of the Great Depression and served as a powerful commander-in-chief who secured victory during World War II. While the media always supported FDR's requests not to be photographed in his wheelchair, supporters of the new statue wanted people to be reminded that it is no longer necessary to hide disabilities. They believe that it helps send a public message that anyone, whatever their ability, gender, language, nationality, or age, can make a positive difference. Acknowledging disability helps fight stereotyping and stigmatization. As a result, on January 10, 2000, President Clinton dedicated this new addition to the Franklin Delano Roosevelt Memorial.

The statue of FDR in a wheelchair, added to the monument after requests by disability advocates. (Photo courtesy Don Ward.)

## Using Compare and Contrast Transition Words to Describe Two Sculptures

The two FDR statues are similar in some ways and different in others. Write down five descriptive sentences about each statue.

| FDR Statue with Cape | FDR Wheelchair Statue |
|---|---|
| *The statue is green.* | *The statue is bronze.* |
| *The statue is detailed.* | *The statue is detailed.* |
| 1. | 1. |
| 2. | 2. |
| 3. | 3. |
| 4. | 4. |
| 5. | 5. |

Learning "compare and contrast" transition words is helpful because they are commonly used by U.S. American English speakers to connect ideas and information about things that are similar and different. Learning to use these words effectively can help you to speak and write more like a native speaker of English. Transition words used for comparing usually point out similarities, whereas transitions used for contrasting point out differences. Here is a list of the most commonly used transition words and phrases for these purposes.

| Compare (Similarity) | Contrast (Difference) |
|---|---|
| similarly | but |
| likewise | however |
| in the same way | yet |
| in a like manner | while |
| by the same token | whereas |
| equally | conversely |
| | on the other hand |

Both compare and contrast transition words are used to connect the ideas of two complete, independent sentences to form a stronger relationship between the sentences. The transition word is used at the beginning of the second sentence.

Example (Comparing): *The FDR statue with cape is detailed. In a like manner, the FDR wheelchair statue is detailed.*

Example (Contrasting): *The FDR statue with cape is green. On the other hand, the FDR wheelchair statue is bronze.*

Use the descriptive sentences you wrote and give examples of comparing and contrasting transition sentences describing the similarities and differences in the FDR statues.

1.

2.

3.

4.

5.

6.

## Expressing and Supporting Our Own Opinions about Public Representation via Memorials

Look at the two statues again. Below are the beginnings of some sentences about the statues. Finish them with your own interpretation(s) of what they each convey to the public.

| 1997 Statue with Cape | 2000 Statue with Wheelchair |
|---|---|
| I believe this statue conveys the message that . . . | I believe this statue conveys the message that . . . |
| I think that the artist created this statue with a cape because . . . | I think that the artist created this statue with a wheelchair because . . . |
| My opinion about the artist's inclusion of a cape is that it . . . | My opinion about the artist's inclusion of a wheelchair is that it . . . |

| 1997 Statue with Cape | 2000 Statue with Wheelchair |
|---|---|
| I feel that this statue is important to people who . . . | I feel that this statue is important to people who . . . |
| I like/dislike this statue because . . . | I like/dislike this statue because . . . |

When people have different opinions, it is often necessary to note whether you agree with some aspect of what the other person is saying, or whether you completely disagree before giving your own opinion. Look at the following chart.

| Yes, but I think that<br>Yes, but I believe that<br>Yes, but I feel that | Show partial agreement with the speech partner's opinion. |
|---|---|
| I disagree because<br>I see it differently because<br>I don't think so because | Show complete disagreement with the speaker's opinion. |

Here is an example of an exchange that shows partial agreement with the speech partner's opinion.

> Speaker One: *I dislike this statue because the wheels on the wheelchair are too big.*
> Speaker Two: *Yes, but I feel that the wheelchair is still important.*

Here is an example of an exchange that shows complete disagreement with the speaker's opinion.

> Speaker One: *I believe that this statue conveys the message that wheelchairs are not publically accepted.*
> Speaker Two: *I disagree because Roosevelt himself did not want to be portrayed in his wheelchair. The statue is respectful of his personal wishes.*

Work with a partner in class using the opinion sentences you completed in the last section. Look at each other's opinions. Which ones do you partially agree with? Which ones do you completely disagree with? Practice responding to each of your partner's sentences using one of the phrases listed in the box on page 153.

**Link to Today**

## Equal Access on Campus—Can Everybody Have a Share?

In 1973, the *Rehabilitation Act* was passed in Congress. This act made it illegal for any organization that received government money to discriminate against disabled persons. In terms of education, the *Individuals with Disabilities Education Act* passed two years later guaranteed free public schooling through high school. However, although the intent was there, many students were still segregated from the mainstream population because of architectural barriers that prevented access to school buildings, such as lack of elevators or wheelchair ramps. The *Americans with Disabilities Act* was signed into law in 1990, requiring that all new and remodeled buildings be accessible to persons with disabilities. This is part of the requirement to provide reasonable accommodation to all students.

Many college campuses have offices that specialize in helping students with a variety of physical and mental impairments, and requests for accommodation are growing. Beyond physical resources such as interpreters for the hearing impaired or note takers for the visually impaired, such offices are being asked for services such as special test-taking accommodations and extra time to complete exams for those who have documented learning disabilities.

## Fast Facts

- In 1999, a student at a California university said she was forced to switch her major from science to English because she could not reach the lab equipment.

- Between 1988 and 1998, the number of freshmen describing themselves as disabled increased 35%—mostly due to claims of learning disabilities.

- Disabled students at a university in Arizona were not included in a fire-drill evacuation plan for their dorm and were directed instead to police and fire officials for assistance.

- An urban college recently expanded a computer lab with equipment for students with learning disabilities, eye problems, and other challenges.

**Positive Aspects of Campus Accessibility**
Find and read a newspaper, magazine, or Internet article on a positive aspect of accessibility issues in public and on campus. Summarize it in your own words.

**Negative Aspects of Campus Accessibility**
Find and read a newspaper, magazine, or Internet article on a negative aspect of accessibility issues in public and on campus. Summarize it in your own words.

**My Personal Conclusion(s) About Campus Accessibility**

## Putting It All Together

Think about what you have learned in this unit and from the activities you did and the discussions you had. Write down your thoughts on the following questions and then share ideas with classmates.

1. What surprised me most about the information on diversity in the United States?

2. What does this information help me to understand about life in the United States?

3. How does knowing this information change my mind about U.S. American values and attitudes?

4. Can people in my community learn something from the experiences U.S. Americans had with diversity?

5. What will I tell people now if they ask me about disabled persons in the United States?

6. What kinds of positive changes can be made regarding accessibility for all people? Should any changes be made at all?

# Comments and Suggestions
for the Teacher

The title of *What Makes America Tick?* is an interesting discussion feature, since it plays on an idiomatic expression. I think students should be familiar with the expression "to find out what makes somebody tick" because it is an important part of the underlying premise of the book, namely that in addition to learning language skills, students can expect to learn a little bit more about what drives members of the target culture. Such a discussion will likely generate interest and curiosity. Students can preview the chapter titles and look through the book to build expectations and try to formulate an initial answer to the overriding question of the course of study: What are the shared values and assumptions springing from the historical, collective cultural consciousness of U.S. Americans that make them act and think the way they do? What *does* make America tick?

As a side note, please make students aware that the phrase is an idiom and does not refer in any official capacity to the study of American culture, economics, politics, etc. I was made aware of this misconception (mostly a phonetic one, I think) when I found out to both my horror and amusement that several of my students had written journal entries to the teacher who was their level advisor that semester about how much fun they were having in *"Americatics"* (*America* + *ticks*). While I was flattered that they would mention it in their journals and pretty impressed with their linguistic ingenuity in doing so, it may help you from the outset to make it clear to students that the course of study outlined in the book is primarily sociolinguistic awareness and language practice in the four skill areas based within the context of the discipline of American cultural studies. EFL teachers especially need to make their students aware of the constraints of such an approach, as it is based heavily in popular culture and cultural artifacts that, while part of the collective consciousness of many Americans, do not systematically represent subcultural and individual concerns that ESL students will have the advantage of encountering more readily in their daily lives while interacting with individuals from the target culture. In other words, although *What Makes America Tick?* is a fairly comprehensive representation of some major historical events and cultural trends in the United States, it in no way can serve as a sum total of every historical and cultural relationship, and students must be reminded that U.S. history and culture is much more complex than that which a textbook of this scope can adequately cover.

I designed *What Makes America Tick?* for intermediate language students as an intelligent alternative to "dumbed-down" and overly simplified teaching materials often created at this level. The book actually grew out of my own anger and disappointment with the materials used in my German as a Second Language classroom in Austria. Having arrived with a BA in German, I was not very happy to find out that classroom materials consisted mainly of "kiddie" activities. I vowed then and there that if I ever became a language teacher, I would do my best to create something engaging for adult learners. I therefore made every effort to design and sell this project as an intermediate text and to keep the kind of language activities and skills needed to complete them at the ACTFL intermediate-level guidelines.

Because the text includes cultural artifacts, there are advanced-level materials contained in the text. However, the activities that learners are asked to engage in with the texts are intermediate per ACTFL guidelines. Such activities include: asking and answering questions; initiating, sustaining and closing conversations; comprehending connected discourse; combining and recombining given elements; and writing narratives, autobiographies, summaries, and paraphrases. You will note that unit activities progress from primarily narrative/descriptive activities and activities that call for question answering and simple recombinations of learned elements to slightly more complex activities involving stating observations to simple hypothesis and opinion support as the units progress. This push into limited ACTFL advanced-level indicators was factored into the book preparation as a conscious push toward lower-end advanced language use and should not be taken as an indicator of initial design for advanced level students.

## Unit Introductions

My main goal with the activities on the unit opening pages is to provide an introduction to the unit, to provide visual stimulation for learners, and to activate prior and/or related knowledge on the topic in a schemata-building manner. The activities are also designed to encourage intermediate speakers to speculate, formulate, and articulate simple hypotheses or express limited opinions without the need for supporting those opinions or using advanced indicators such as subjunctive case. This can serve to prepare intermediate students for more systematic advanced usage. The photo on each unit title page is intended to be used for schemata-building, brainstorming, and discussing ideas and engaging in information-gap activities and communicative work.

## Net Surfers, Presidential Suite, On TV, Music Box, At the Movies

**Net Surfers** is comprised of a list of pretested Internet search terms bringing up Web sites that are related to the content of each unit. Because URLs change so rapidly, I thought that providing the tools for fruitful Internet searching would be more helpful than listing actual URLs themselves. The **Presidential Suite** accompanies the time line and gives an idea of who was president during the time that the chapter events were taking place. **On TV, Music Box,** and **At the Movies** all provide a few suggestions for authentic media realia related to the topics or eras covered in the unit that learners can watch or listen to in their free time; the lists are not meant to be exhaustive. This is also intended as a potential classroom resource, since permissions and copyright issues prevented them from being included more systematically in the curriculum.

## Preparing to Read about . . .

This brief overview of each unit seeks to provide learners with schemata-building foreshadowing that provides both a content summary and context for understanding the unit as it relates to preceding and following units. Students are asked to do a self-reflective or interview activity based on the major concepts that will appear later. This serves both schemata-building and information-gap functions. Since students are asked to relate main concepts to themselves and their own experiences, personal information may be brought up in this setting. Each unit contains a reminder to students that they are in no way obligated to share information in public that they feel uncomfortable about. It is my belief that in making personal connections to texts and ideas, both personal and linguistic risks are taken. We as teachers should provide a safe place for that sort of risk-taking by assuring our students that they, as adult learners, are both able and allowed to choose for themselves what information will be shared through language.

## Learning New Vocabulary about . . .

 The words chosen for each unit are mostly high-frequency words and derivatives taken from Bauman and Culligan's 1995 frequency-adapted General Service List. The 2284-word list is derived from West's (1953) General Service List, Bauer and Nation's (1995) headword concept, and frequency numbers from the Brown Corpus (Frances and Kucera 1982). Unit vocabulary also highlights to some degree key concept words specific to U.S. American history and ideology. Whether vocabulary is pretaught or taught in conjunction with or even after the reading is left to the individual teacher. Research supports both approaches at the intermediate level, and the best approach may vary from class to class and even from student to student. In any case, vocabulary is a major component of the concept of the book and should be accorded a proportionate amount of time. Difficult vocabulary from cultural artifacts such as novels is glossed since these are included as demonstrations of language use influenced by history in cultural products. Learners are also encouraged to guess at words in context and to read for holistic comprehension without knowing every vocabulary word.

## Talking about New Words and Ideas

I designed this section to give learners the opportunity to relate key new words/concepts to their own personal lives and to create personal synonym lists for certain vocabulary words. The learner is provided with information as to why the concept is important in the United States. Then the learner focuses on his/her own interactions with the concept by reflecting about how (whether) these concepts operate in their communities and how (whether) these concepts operate in the students' own personal frameworks. Such discussion is genuine and authentic, information-gap and communicative. It also serves as a further schemata-building activity for the reading. Again, the activity can be done after the reading if the class/teacher prefers it, but it is suggested that it come before the reading. I recommend small group work rather than large class discussion (at least initially).

## Making Predictions about the Reading

All good readers make predictions about the texts they are about to encounter, whether those predictions are correct or not. Each unit contains prediction-making activities, explaining why it is important. Because this is an easily worn-out and repetitive activity, I made conscious efforts to include activities such as discussing, comparing notes, altering assumptions based on new information obtained during comparison, and slightly increased negotiation demands as the units progress. I believe that in addition to providing pedagogically sound prereading activities, this section also fosters the kind of discussion that lays a foundation for more advanced linguistic skill indicators.

## Reading about . . .

The reading passages are designed to be challenging and will need to be given adequate time in the classroom. While I clearly focused the textbook on intermediate learners, I designed the vocabulary and sentence structures in the text to stretch the intermediate learner. I feel that the discussion of abstract historical concepts should occur in an accessible yet intelligent manner. While the resulting materials may seem intimidating at first, I assure you that ACTFL reading guidelines for intermediate abilities were adhered to closely during the writing and revision stages of the text, especially those regarding the use of grammatical forms related to advanced use such as subjunctives and hypothetical theses. Intermediate-mid and intermediate-advanced ACTFL guidelines in reading state that the student can understand and respond to texts in which the main ideas are presented via description and narration. They can also deal effectively with texts that address a variety of social needs and that activate schemata. While the sentence structure in the readings becomes more complex and varied as the chapters progress, there is nothing represented in the reading passages that cannot be processed cognitively by the intermediate adult learner. With special attention to key vocabulary and a "can do" attitude on the part of the learner and teacher, the reading activities should prove to be one of the main factors in helping the learner along the path from intermediate to more advanced usage.

## Responding to Information about . . .

I am particularly happy with this section, which I designed to give learners the opportunity to engage in global interaction with the text before being asked to demonstrate discrete point comprehension. I added this section toward the final stages of revising the manuscript based on classroom action research that inquires into the reading processes of L1 learners. This shows that students who are asked to make connections between texts and themselves, texts and other texts, and texts and the world around them as well as inferences such as imagery, conclusions, predictions, and synthesis learn to become more competent readers than students who are asked to merely respond to comprehension checks. I would like to acknowledge and thank Ellin Oliver Keene and Susan Zimmermann for recording their classroom experiences and for inspiring this section of the textbook.

## Understanding the Reading: Comprehension Check

I designed this section with a dual purpose: (1) to make sure that learners understand the key points of the readings, as they are necessary to understanding information from the rest of the chapter, and (2) to introduce students to various evaluation techniques that are likely to be encountered in the U.S. academic setting. I chose to present evaluation tools as a cultural construct, highlighting their reasons for use, as well as the "tricks" to better maneuvering them.

## Authentic Cultural Material Activity

These activities vary from unit to unit but have the common goal of exposing the learner to an original cultural artifact such as an excerpt from a famous speech or novel, a piece of artwork or advertisement, etc., with emphasis on one or more of the language skills. In addition to serving as a tangible representative cultural product of the historical, factual materials presented in the readings, these artifacts are also used in the units as a springboard to linguistic exercises that focus on the way in which language is used by native speakers to achieve communicative goals to a larger audience.

## "About Our Own Experience" Activities

I designed these activities as spin-offs from the Authentic Cultural Material Activity to give intermediate-level language users an opportunity to express themselves meaningfully and to create with their level of linguistic resources. Although this section generally focuses on a specific linguistic structure, I did not conceptualize it as a grammar/structure section per se. Rather, I choose to highlight the link between cultural and pragmatic awareness. Sociolinguistic competency, or at the very least, an awareness of it via cultural materials, is the main goal outcome of this section. I feel strongly that students should have the opportunity to "publish" the work created during these activities. For example, in Unit 4, a speech day can be held in class. As the students listen to a recording, attention can be given to the strength and conviction in Martin Luther King, Jr.'s voice as he delivers his speech. Students can then give their "I Have a Dream" speeches, focusing on speaking strongly and clearly. Other classroom publishing opportunities can be created by the use of "wall newspapers" in the hallway or a "language gallery" in the classroom.

## Link to Today

This feature is perhaps the most important one of the textbook and the one of which I am the most proud. I designed Link to Today with the intent of drawing an explicit connection between cultural artifacts, historical events, and current values of U.S. Americans. This section consists of a brief explanation of the current situation and its relationship to the historical one. Short excerpts and story lines featuring actual U.S. citizens from more recent newspapers, opinion polls, magazines, etc., are presented along with various opinions and activities that are offshoots of the original historical event discussed. There are no formal activities linked with this section. I present it to you, the teacher, and your students to be used in whatever manner you find most useful, either as an informational activity, an impetus for discussion, or the basis for further projects.

Since many of the Link to Today topics are controversial and fall outside of the norms of what may be addressed in the classroom in the home cultures of many students, I would like to give you some general advice for this section. I feel that it is extremely important to both introduce and reinforce to students that the U.S. is a very heterogeneous society with many opinions and viewpoints represented. The excerpts chosen for this section replicate this multiplicity, and I made every effort to give voice to varying sides of and opinions about the issue. It may help to explain that culturally, U.S. Americans are educated and socialized from an early age to respect the opinions, viewpoints, and practices of others while being proud of and strong in their own. It may also help to validate the possibility that the viewpoints expressed by U.S. Americans may not be representative of the ones held by the students. It should also be made clear that the information is given only to help in the process of understanding the variety of current values and beliefs, not to force students to take sides on any issue presented. In addition, you may want to inform the students that teachers in U.S. American educational institutions are discouraged from and generally don't give personal opinions in the classroom as part of the practice of encouraging individual students to formulate their own opinions, just as I have not included my personal opinions in the student portions of the textbook.

I believe that an atmosphere of respect for all reactions to the issues portrayed and one that encourages but does not enforce the articulation of opinions in the classroom is the most conducive to meeting the goals of the Link to Today sections. When the value of each individual contribution is recognized and when students understand that there is no right or wrong answers to these issues (including the teacher's), their willingness to speak and share ideas should increase, thereby resulting in more authentic language practice. As always, students who do not wish to deal with certain issues brought up in these sections should not be forced to do so.

## Putting It All Together

This section provides a capstone to the activities presented throughout the unit and is designed to allow learners to process the information in its entirety and to reflect upon how they understand the information and how they interact with it. It provides learners with the opportunity to reflect how the gained knowledge will be used upon return to the home culture or upon further integration into the target culture. The progression of questions in this section was originally conceptualized as a midterm exam and elicited consistently positive responses from students. It makes the testing of detailed, factual information more valid by integrating it with personal understanding. Therefore, along with a leading question that asks students to explain the factual events of the unit in as much detail as possible, any or all of the questions in this section could be used for short answer/essay exams.

# Answer Key

## Unit 1 Understanding the Reading: Comprehension Check

| immigration | growing cities |
|---|---|
| bribery | factory owners |
| agriculture | farmers |
| Mother Jones | child laborers |
| muckrakers | newspaper reporters |
| prohibition | alcohol drinkers |
| suffrage | women |

### Language Focus: Using Suggestion Phrases

There is room for some negotiation and disagreement on this, but a general order from least to most strong looks somewhat like this.

| | |
|---|---|
| It's a good idea to | Let's |
| You might want to | You should |
| You could | You ought to |
| Why don't you | (You must) |

## Unit 2 Understanding the Reading: Comprehension Check

| | | |
|---|---|---|
| passenger | progressive | help Americans |
| itself | rejected | jobs and hope |
| wild | panicked | socialist |
| fun | destroyed | helped |
| dances, movies, and music | unemployment and homelessness | |

## Unit 3   Understanding the Reading: Comprehension Check

1. False. While these were the two most notable and far-reaching changes, they were not the *only* ones.
2. False. It was a concept upon which the nation was founded. Consumer culture enhanced the idea and made it more tangible to people.
3. True.
4. False. The middle class began to grow.
5. True
6. False. Many people, especially older ones, rejected his music. (Note that "everybody" is derived from "every.")
7. True

## Unit 4   Understanding the Reading: Comprehension Check

1. b
2. c
3. a
4. a
5. a
6. c
7. d
8. a
9. d
10. c

## Unit 5   Understanding the Reading: Comprehension Check

(Students may use any words that demonstrate understanding of the text.)

### Using Less Direct Speech in Making Requests

There is room for some negotiation and disagreement on this, but a general order from most direct to least direct looks like this.

"Put the money in the bag!"
"You'd better give me some money!"
"Give me money!"
"I need some money."
"May I have some of your money?"
"Could you lend me some money?"
"Would it be possible for you to lend me some money?"

Assuming normal relations, one would be the least direct with a stranger, more direct with a librarian as he/she is in a service position, and most direct with a friend. Polite interaction with everybody is, however, still expected no matter what the level of formality.

### Applying What We've Learned from *On the Road: Traveling Route 66*

From east to west, Route 66 passes through these major cities and states:

Chicago, Illinois
Springfield, Illinois
St. Louis, Missouri
Tulsa, Oklahoma
Oklahoma City, Oklahoma
Amarillo, Texas
Sante Fe, New Mexico
Albuquerque, New Mexico
Flagstaff, Arizona
Los Angeles, California

Route 66 also passes through a corner of Kansas.

### Unit 6   Understanding the Reading: Comprehension Check

1. The U.S. and the Soviet Union were competing in an arms race, the space race, and the ideological conflict between communism and democracy.
2. Americans believed that like a disease, communism was contagious and would spread.
3. McCarthyism was a heightened anticommunist feeling in the United States led by Senator Joseph McCarthy.
4. The U.S. invested monetary aid in countries threatened by communism such as West Germany (Berlin) and South Vietnam.
5. The domino effect states that if one country becomes communist, so will the countries surrounding it.
6. The U.S. believed that South Vietnam would become communist because North Vietnam and neighboring countries had, so the U.S. became involved in the war.
7. JFK sent military advisors and tried to maintain stability; LBJ intensified the war effort but continued to deny that the U.S. was involved in war.
8. The Vietnam War caused large-scale protests and political upheaval in the United States.

### Applying Our Understanding to Order Events in History

1. World War II ends, leaving two superpowers in the world with opposing economic systems and ideologies.
2. The United States sends military and monetary aid to areas of the world threatened by communism.
3. A civil war erupts in Vietnam.
4. Presidents Eisenhower and Kennedy send "military advisors" to Vietnam to help South Vietnam remain stable.

5. President John F. Kennedy is assassinated. Vice President Lyndon B. Johnson is sworn in as president.
6. Congress passes the Tonkin Gulf Resolution, allowing President Johnson to officially order bombing raids against North Vietnam.
7. The draft threatens many young men and some leave the U.S. for Canada.
8. Richard M. Nixon is elected president of the United States.
9. 100,000 people march in Washington, D.C., to show the government what they think of the war.
10. Protesting at Kent State University in Ohio leaves four students dead and nine wounded.
11. Vietnam Veterans are scorned and disrespected upon their return from the war.
12. The Vietnam Veterans Memorial is built and dedicated.

## Language Focus: Understanding Poetry and Figurative Meaning

*Dictionary Definition*

crenelated (adj). 1. Having battlements 2. Indented, notched

*Literal Meaning*

| Name | Home State | Description |
|---|---|---|
| Lonnie | Tennessee | He has had an arm amputation. |
| Danny | California (Los Angeles) | He has been blinded. |
| Chief the Ute | no information | He has become a "partial" man; possible amputation or impotence. |
| Pocho | Arizona | He wanted to hear words in his mother tongue, presumably Spanish. |
| Skeets | no information | He wanted to hear the words to the popular hymn "Amazing Grace." |
| boy with no name | no information | He has no voice and no face; he represents the anonymous masses of soldiers. |

*Figurative Meaning*

1. Allusion

This is open to discussion and interpretation, but here are some ideas.

| Dana Schuster | Emily Dickinson |
|---|---|
| tucks names into her heart | tucks poems into the wall |
| thinks and writes about her memories and ideas | thinks and writes about her memories and ideas |
| wears green of an army uniform while working | wears white while working |
| spent time working in a hospital dealing with physical illness | spent time under medical evaluation for mental illness (for agoraphobia: fear of being in public and other anxieties) |

The other allusion in the text is to the hymn "Amazing Grace."

2. Language register

The example of a change in language register is the sentence in verse 2 of the poem: "Don't mean nothin'. I got another one." Why the poet uses this shift in language is open to speculation, but it possibly serves to illustrate the rawness of emotion that the amputation has caused in the man who spoke the words.

3. Metaphor

| Writing Metaphor | Housecleaning Metaphor |
|---|---|
| perhaps to edit | when alcoves need airing |
| perhaps to erase | when corners need cleaning |

## Unit 7   Understanding the Reading: Comprehension Check

Check for rewriting the main ideas of the reading in students' own words.

## Unit 8   Understanding the Reading: Comprehension Check

Check for retelling the main ideas of the reading in students' own words.